Ageing Gracefully

The Art of Living Well, Longer

DR. JAY DAS

Clever Fox Publishing
Chennai • Bangalore

CLEVER FOX PUBLISHING
Chennai, India

Published by CLEVER FOX PUBLISHING 2025

ISBN: 978-93-7500-217-8

Dr Jay immigrated to Australia from India in July 1971 to undertake his PhD studies in biochemistry. He then joined the pharmaceutical industry via multinational corporations, Fisons and 3M, where he successfully developed a broad range of pharmaceutical products and researched their medical application.

After a chance meeting with the late Bob Lucy, one of the pioneers in advancing the use of nutritional supplements in Australia, Dr Jay successfully transitioned to natural therapies working across research and development, manufacturing and quality control. He retired from commercial assignments as a General Manager at the age of 52 and started his own company with various interests. He continues to be involved in the industry, but in a much less involved way.

Now at the age of 76, Dr Jay intends to share the knowledge he has gained from over 45 years of experience in the health and wellness industry.

After completing his first book successfully, Dr. Jay has embarked upon writing books on several topics relating to Age and Well-being and eventually hopes to publish them in due course. This, his second book, is based on seniors in our community and the ageing process and he firmly believes that Ageing Gracefully is every senior's right and expectation.

To all my fellow seniors who have inspired me throughout my journey into the ageing process. Keep well and healthy and Age gracefully through your life's journey.

Dr. Jayanto (Jay) Das (Ph.D.)
*Former Fellow of the Royal Society of Health (FRSH, London)
and Royal Australian Chemical Institute (RACI, Australia)*

Ageing Gracefully

(Healthy Ageing with Style, Vitality and Purpose)

Writing a book on any subject matter has not been an easy task. There are many considerations that need to be addressed and finalised for inclusion. There are several issues which need to be resolved, checked and verified before the manuscript is put together for the first reading. Also, many people in the background must be acknowledged, as the task I have undertaken cannot be made possible without their help. There are a few people who have encouraged me throughout this process; my family, even my little grandsons, played an important role; just their presence has been an inspiration as they are part of a healthy future.

Some of my colleagues, many of whom I had many a discussion with on the subject of nutrition and general well-being had nothing but encouraged me. My niece, Dr. Anjana Poddar, who did the first reading of the manuscript and provided valuable suggestions. To my son Sandeep Das for his expertise on nutrition and also on movements and exercises.

The Publishers, Clever Fox Publishing, who helped me with the editing, layouts, designing, printing and publishing the book, have done a wonderful professional job.

Finally, to all seniors who are a constant source of inspiration to me. But most of all, to all of you out there, who I hope will read the book not as a textbook but as a fun read. My sincere wish and hope is that people who read this book will gain some health awareness and consciousness to live a long, healthy and happy life and to carers who share the immense responsibility of caring for the seniors I wish to thank them for their commitment and dedication in the area of seniors' care and health management.

Please read the book and enjoy the journey, as I have enjoyed writing for you.

Contents

Preface

I have been tempted to write a book on Nutrition, health and ageing for quite some time and luckily, an opportunity came up after I had finished my previous book *"Let your Organs Breathe"*, which I was told was a successful project. I had started working on *"Let your Organs Breathe"* during the Covid-19 lockdown towards the end of 2020, which was an advantage time-wise. But with my new project, time became an issue amidst other projects I was involved in. As I am 76 and looking forward to the years ahead, a lot of thoughts have crossed my mind and a burning question remains: how am I going to handle old age? I am sure there are many of us in this elite age group of ours who at certain times of their life have also thought of the same issue. Handling old age can be a bit stressful as we are embarking on an unknown journey. It can be simple yet daunting when laws of Nature take over the "human lifecycle". But now, having crossed the threshold in my journey and making the transition from a so-called active old age with a busy lifestyle, I feel quite comfortable and at home. And, having spent more than a decade in this new uncharted territory (for me), I know my best years are ahead of me and I am looking forward to it with a very positive outlook, come what may.

To handle the process of getting old and balancing all life's factors pertaining to our individual circumstances, it can be challenging and stressful, but we have to find our own enlightened path through this maze, that we call the lifecycle, which takes us through various stages of life. It is a fact of life that we are born to get old one day and eventually pass on. How we manage and control the sequence of events of growing old is entirely up to us; it is an individual perception since we cannot stop getting old, it is an inevitable fact of life.

Ancient philosophers and physicians thought of the ageing process as the most crucial stage of our lifelong journey and linked each stage of old age with possible health conditions.

Galen (129AD – 216AD), in his treatise "Hygiene," emphasized healthy ageing with nutrition and exercise and wrote the importance of hygiene as an important factor in growing old. His views carry a lot of significance to this day and become a basis for healthy living.

Many ancient philosophers of their time had different spins on getting old, but they all had a common theme, which revolved around good nutrition and exercise and this is going to be a consolidation of my book on ageing gracefully.

Bertrand Russell, one of the great philosophers and lateral thinkers of modern times, says about old age, "Make your interests gradually wider and more impersonal, until bit by bit the walls of the ego recede, and your life becomes increasingly merged in the universal life."

"The man who, in old age, can see his life in this way, will not suffer from the fear of death, since the things he cares for will continue. And if, with the decay of vitality, weariness increases, the thought of rest will not be unwelcome. I should wish to die while still at work, knowing that others will carry on what I can no longer do and content in the thought that what was possible has been done". **Bertrand Russell** (b. May 18, 1872– d. February 2, 1970).

What a simple perspective on getting old, and this is what I call "Ageing Gracefully".

About the Book

The idea for Ageing Gracefully was conceived a few years ago when I jumped all the hurdles and landed in my 70s still healthy and going strong. I felt good about it and made a resolution that I must write a book on Ageing Gracefully. Sometimes ideas come dime a dozen, Covid-19 struck the world, and we started having lockdowns and several social restrictions imposed on us, mind you, for our own good as the experts would have us believe.

During the lockdown period of late 2020, around December, I started working on my first book *"Let your Organs Breathe,"* a book on Nutrition, tweaked with a bit of philosophy to make it a fun read and to spread awareness of nutrition which I still think lacks general awareness in the public domain. It took me almost eighteen months to two years to complete.

Ageing gracefully is really a subject close to my heart as I am in the running for it, sorry running with it. Physical ageing starts in our early 70s when we start to look old-ish in our appearance. Our hair starts to turn grey and may even shed a few strands of hair follicles. Just like seasonal change when trees begin to shed old leaves in preparation for spring, bearing new leaves and colourful blossoms. The only difference is that fallen leaves from trees regrow, while our fallen or lost hair will not and there will be a void. Other attributes of getting old are our integumentary system (our skin) starts to sag, wrinkles begin to appear and creaking joints, aches and pains take over. We start to think that we are not young anymore.

While all this is happening, we occasionally come across senior citizens who are blessed with that eternal youthful look and charm, indeed the envy of all of us, somewhat in a good way, as we can draw inspiration from those members of our elite seniors group. While the book touches on scientific concepts, they are presented in a clear and accessible manner. The occasional use of science is measured and purposeful, offered not to overwhelm, but to empower. Readers are gently guided through the "why' behind the wellness strategies, ensuring a deeper and more meaningful understanding of how to age well.

This book, I hope, will spread the word to all seniors that we do still have a lot to contribute to society; our biggest weaponry in our arsenal is our wisdom and years of experience. One good thing that happened out of the pandemic (COVID-19) was that many of us got the opportunity to present our skills, apply them in the right place at the right time and most of all to share our experiences with the workforce in general. Through this book, my sincere wish is to promote healthy ageing to my fellow senior citizens, not only from the nutritional point of view but also from the personal hygiene and healthy living and also to be aware of the factors that can affect Graceful ageing. We all can fight the negatives and bring out the positives to enlighten our path to old age and live happily and gracefully till our time is up on this wonderful planet of ours, we call home. There are several key words and phrases that ornament this book, reflecting the philosophy and strategies that define the journey of *Ageing Gracefully*. These ideas are cultivated throughout the chapters and form the foundation for living with vitality, dignity, and purpose.

Healthy ageing and seniors' wellness emphasise a well-rounded lifestyle for older adults—often an overlooked group—founded on three essential pillars: nourishing diet and nutrition, regular physical activity, and meaningful social interaction. Together, these elements support physical, mental, and emotional well-being in later years. Closely linked to this is the concept of mind. Body and health, which recognises that true wellness cannot exist without harmony between the mind, body, and soul. With as many as 14% to 25% of adults globally over 60, experiencing mental health challenges, often untreated, re-enforces this interdependence for ageing well. Support systems from family, friends, and community are essential and equally vital. They offer emotional stability, reduce the feeling of loneliness, and foster a sense of belonging. All of which are indispensable for resilience and healthy ageing. Alongside this, ageing with purpose is a guiding principle. Rather than seeing ageing as a decline. This phase of life can be a time of renewal, contribution to society, and self-discovery. This is consistent with developing skills to explore new interests, share wisdom and live with dignity. Holistic ageing brings all these positives together and encourages a complete approach to *Ageing Gracefully* that integrates physical, emotional, social, and spiritual health. It is a reminder that holistic wellness is not just the absence of disease and disappointments but the presence of balance, mindfulness, and meaningful engagement with life and an appreciation of our ageing process.

My one request to my readers is, please do not use this book as a textbook but as a fun read to enjoy and enhance your awareness of growing old.

Please read the book and make the journey to "Ageing Gracefully" with me.

Disclaimer: This book is written in good faith as a fun read and not as a textbook. The author has attempted to verify all facts used in the book, but does not guarantee its validity; readers must use their own discretion when using any part of the book. For all the references used, the author is grateful, and, no copyright infringement is intended. If I have failed to acknowledge any reference that I have used in the book, it is not intentional and I humbly apologise for it.

Finally, never neglect medical advice given to you by your doctor and your physician, but rather follow that advice for your own good.

Read my book, enjoy and age gracefully.

Chapter 1

OLD AGE AND "HUMAN LIFECYCLE"

"Life begins in the safe cradle of our mother's womb and ends in the eternal embrace of Mother Nature."

– Jay Das 2024

To define ageing, we need to understand the lifecycle of human beings.

Human life cycle:

The human life cycle begins from the copulation stage after an adult male sperm successfully fertilizes the female egg in the womb, facilitating the pathway to a beautiful beginning of human life. It is more complex than said, and follows a sequence of various biological developmental stages from foetus to old age finally ending in our death thus completing the cycle.

On average, the cycle consists of 80-85 years; more or less.

In this 85-year life span, we grow up from a tiny life form in our mother's womb to an old person who has achieved a full lifetime of accomplishment and is now preparing for their eternal journey. Lifetime achievements vary widely from individual to individual and so does our life span.

When we look back and observe our life cycle, an interesting truth emerges. We spend nearly 35 to 40 years building careers, accumulating experiences, and striving toward our goals and glory. Thereafter, only about 20 years remain to actually enjoy the rewards of our earlier efforts. And within those final years, the last 5 years, we live with memories. But unfortunately for some, even those memories may slip away.

How did I arrive at this perspective? Typically, we complete our formal education by the age of 20-25 years and settle into our chosen profession by 30 years of age. From this time on until the common retirement age of 65, we spend about 35 years of a productive, professionally fulfilling life. After our retirement age of 65 years, assuming good health, we might look forward to 10 or 15 years of retirement, hopefully living our lives in good health, wellness, reflection, and joy.

But those later years are often shaped by our earlier choices. According to current data, about 20% of people aged 65 and above experience mild cognitive decline, and nearly 5 million Americans in that age group are living with Alzheimer's disease. (www.everydayhealth.com/news/most-common-health-concerns-seniors) These numbers aren't meant to alarm but to awaken us.

The message is clear. Longevity does not just mean how long we live; it is not about quantity but quality.

And this begins with a holistic approach and embracing practices that support sustained health and graceful aging.

Similar statistics were reported by the Australian Institute of Health and Awareness (Sep. 2022) which reported that there are almost 83 people with dementia per 1,000 Australians aged 65 and over and nearly two-thirds of these Australians with dementia are women (https://www.dementia.org.au/statistics).

Ageing gracefully is simply a philosophy (in my humble opinion) of positive thoughts and actions. It is the most powerful tool in our old age to provide us with that extra push, to battle on and live the rest of our life with dignity, grace and good health. Many of us ignore the opportunity to age gracefully, it is a privilege that we all should embrace. Statistically, it was found that people who are optimists and positive-minded live longer (by 11-15% longer) than those who practice less positive thinking and are less optimistic (study done in 2019, published Wednesday in the Journal of the American Geriatrics Society).

It is also reported *(Jane Strommen, NDSU Extension Gerontology Specialist, 701-231-5948)* that happy people with a positive outlook live longer by 7.5 years. These people had a higher rate of recovery from illness and injuries, had a greater will to live and had a greater control of their lives and also had an improved memory performance. They also looked after themselves by taking regular health check-ups and participating in preventive health care.

Every stage of our development from the foetal stage in our mother's womb to the time or age we finally pass on has a specific time frame.

From a foetus to a well-developed child being born usually takes 36 weeks to 40 weeks. As time slowly passes, the newborn child develops physically with the growth and functions of various organs taking place at a remarkable rate. At this time, the bone structure develops strongly to support the child's developing body and frame. The child has now laid the blueprint of the skeletomuscular system for future years. With each progressing day the child learns various life activities e.g. speaking, walking and running, eating etc. and by the end of 4th year of its life the child is about to take his or her first step into the outside world going to kindergarten, playschools and other child care centres. During this time the child learns more complex emotional and psychological skills with developing brain and other physical attributes.

Let us skip about 6–8 years in a child's lifecycle as these years are spent in further development of the child's already developing physiological and psychological progress. Heading into puberty and young adulthood is perhaps the most interesting developmental period in a child's lifecycle. This is the time when a child, both boys and girls, develop many attributes of young adulthood with physiological and psychological changes. Also, they experience emotions from their wants and needs point of view and experience significant anatomical development. This is the point where a girl and a boy develops a sense of curiosity about their anatomical development and changes and start to ponder over birds and bees. In other words, get attracted to the opposite sex; this is also the time when their sexual preferences take hold, and they become more conscious of their physicality, appearance, and succumb to peer pressures and social influences.

There are several stages from puberty to young adulthood e.g., Adolescence, early Adulthood, etc., when boys and girls in their teens experience more social interactions, impulsive behaviours, risk-taking and their love for privacy, independence and decision making. There are a few negative experiences in a teenager's life at this age such as unruly behaviour, getting on the wrong side of the law, drug and alcohol abuse, and other anti-social activities which can lead their life to destruction which may even scar them for life. A mentoring programme can often bring them back into the straight and narrow path to self-realization and constructive outlooks for a brighter future.

In their late teens, they become interested in jobs and earning an income to sustain their independent lifestyle and explore their identity. After their 21st birthday, the child grows up into full adulthood with abilities to move forward with responsibility and focus on the future.

Adulthood spanning from 21 – 60 years is a big chunk of our life cycle. We start to consolidate our views on life, career, relationships and other activities that distinguish us from our earlier stages of life. Socially, we become more aware and develop a more respectable view of ourselves and become more assertive. A significant portion of our time is taken up in developing partnerships, love interests, work and social tie-ups in the early adulthood phase, say between the years mid to late 20s to late 30s. Marriage, and establishing our own families and consolidation of our nests (and nest eggs), becomes a high priority. We are possibly at the peak of our anatomical and physiological shape in body and mind. At 40 and over, we consolidate our careers and try to carve a niche for ourselves in society, plan ahead for the future, our children's education, and focus on our goals and commitments, and record our achievements. As young parents, we get more involved with our nuclear family.

There are several factors that determine our paths, responsibilities and involvements. Socio-economic situations, personal circumstances and also our ethnicity have a huge impact on how our plans work out in the game of life in the adulthood phase. In the Western society, it is mainly the nuclear family where Father, Mother and their children are of main concern and importance. Although grandparents staying in the background are always of significance to their grandchildren and vice versa. Extension beyond this structure is also a family but the nucleus of the family (the father) may not be responsible or structurally (within the extended family) be as close as that of his own nuclear family.

In many families, some with ethnic backgrounds, it is a loosely tied extended family where grandparents have a special significance to the entire family and not just to their grandchildren. A son or a daughter may consider it his or her partial responsibility to care for their aged parents or another close relative; this in essence, constitutes a part of their extended family. In some descriptions, young parents have come to be known as a sandwich generation, where the young parents due to the overloading of their responsibilities towards their off springs, aged parents, work and social commitments, may find themselves in an overwhelming situation and feel compressed like the meat in the sandwich. But solutions are at hand when grandparents step in and share a bit of the parental role in exchange for their added security, loving family, and basic independent living.

Within our society, one of the main concerns is to address ageing; at what age group should we be identified as, senior or aged! According to the United Nations, (UNO), at the age of 65, we are classified as aged. According to statistics, this is the threshold in our period of life when the rate of sickness, infirmity and even death begins to be of prime concern.

From an article published by the World Health Organization (*WHO, Ageing and Health, October 1, 2022*) I get the feeling that at the age of 60 one qualifies as being old. How was this arrived at?

According to statistics in 2020, the global population of 60 years and over was around 1 billion, and this is predicted to go up to 1.4 billion by 2030 and to 2.1 billion by 2050. Let's look at this age group. Should the population in the age group of 60 years be called old? I don't think so. The majority of this age group are reasonably healthy, have a direction in life and are more focused on the journey ahead. Let's be a bit more open with the description of the elderly and age groups. I tend to think old age starts at the age when we make the transition from our working life to retirement. Some people retire early, hoping to enjoy life when the going is still good. However, some retire late due to financial insecurity and/or other reasons. Again, some may enjoy working in their profession, loving it and therefore retire late. Whatever the situation may be I believe that a person 70 years of age and above should be known as elderly and accorded with every benefit that is available to them.

When we age, we should consider two ageing parameters: one is our biological age and the other is chronological age. What are these you may ask? Simply explained our chronological age is the age calculated from when we are born. Biological age is heavily dependent on our anatomy and physiology and also on psychological issues that may have a profound effect on our development, especially mental and physical. We all may have noticed that some people, both male and female, look more weary and worn out compared to similar-aged people. This may have philosophised the saying "You are as old as you feel".

Every individual has issues and problems in life and has different levels of coping. People who can cope better come out on top and for them, the chronological and biological ages match; this is the essence of ageing gracefully.

Socio-economic status and ageing (SES and A):

Ageing is a very important and delicate phase of our lives. Throughout our working life, we tend to our families and try to make ends meet with the resources available to us. Some are lucky to have saved up a healthy nest egg to provide for us in the future non-productive years (from a financial point of view). There are several factors to it e.g., professional assistance to make the nest egg grow and the more it grows the more secure the future can be. It is important to understand that our socioeconomic status is subject to and dependent on other relevant factors such as education, opportunities available, privileges, social hierarchy and understanding of the socio-economic structure in our society. How this affects the lives of millions of older people in the world is a genuine question that the authorities and the society collectively must address. How is the big unknown here? The population among older age citizens around the world is increasing and bound to increase steadily with the passing of time. We are living longer but whether there is an improvement in the quality of our longevity is subject to debate both in the improved and poorer nations. The SES and A has a multiple and complex facet which has a profound effect on seniors' health and well-being. These are too numerous to enunciate in detail as each factor is a much specialised subject and must be attended to in the proper context. But, to keep a continuity in the present topic of interest, let's recognise a few such as the effect of lower socio-economic status and acceleration in age, impact on cognitive health and so on. Old age is the final stage of our life cycle, the tell-tale signs that we have aged beyond our normal healthy life are when we begin to feel lethargic, a consistent feeling of unwell with aches and pains and joint immobility, problems with our movements, etc. We tend to be unstable, followed by trips and falls and most of all our reliance on others increases dramatically. With SES and A there is a marked impact on our cognitive abilities, impairments in many of our sensory faculties and suffering from major diseases like dementia and depression, chronic obstructive pulmonary disease (COPDS) and many other debilitating diseases like renal and heart diseases. Unfortunately, our socio-economic status adds to our old age diseases and impairments.

But it is not all doom and gloom.

Human Life-cycle

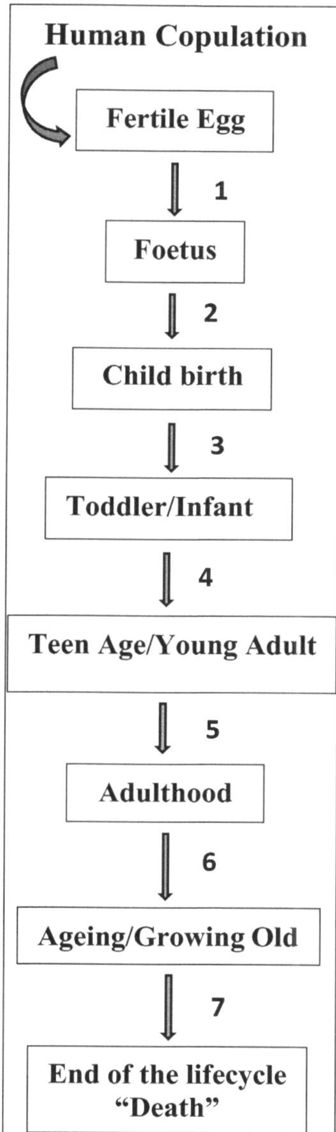

The Seven Ages of Man

All the world's a stage,
And all the men and women merely players:
They have their exits and their entrances;
And one man in his time plays many parts,
His acts being seven ages.
At first the infant,
Mewling and puking in the nurse's arms.
And then the whining schoolboy, with his
satchel,
And shining morning face, creeping like snail
Unwillingly to school.
And then the lover,
Sighing like furnace, with a woeful ballad
Made to his mistress' eyebrow.
Then a soldier,
Full of strange oaths, and bearded like the pard,
Jealous in honour, sudden and quick in quarrel,
Seeking the bubble reputation
Even in the cannon's mouth.
And then the justice,
In fair round belly with good capon lined,
With eyes severe and beard of formal cut,
Full of wise saws and modern instances;
And so, he plays his part.
The sixth age shifts
Into the lean and slippered pantaloon,
With spectacles on nose and pouch on side,
His youthful hose well saved, a world too wide
For his shrunk shank; and his big manly voice,
Turning again toward childish treble, pipes
And whistles in his sound.
Last scene of all,
That ends this strange eventful history,
Is second childishness, and mere oblivion,
Sans teeth, sans eyes, sans taste, sans everything.

William Shakespeare
(From. *As You Like It*)

Old age offers us a lot of time to prepare for this wonderful period of our life, when we can contemplate on our past and plan ahead for our future. Contemplation is a nicely rounded, complete word that allows us to reflect on our past without being judgemental, but allows us to learn from our past mistakes and to prepare for the future. One very important thing I can have an opinion on is "retire gracefully but not inactively". There are so many things we can occupy ourselves with, some of which we can look at towards the end of the chapter.

It is true that as time passes, the aged population around us will increase, as age does not stand still for anyone so there must be a way to standardise the age of a person to enter the elite and graceful seniors group.

To me, "Ageing gracefully is the new inspiration; it is a privilege that only my fellow seniors can enjoy and others can only aspire to".

As we grow old we lose a lot of our body functions, which happens gradually. Our social responsibilities and social interactions also decrease and we become lonelier, not unless there is a strong family support where the grandchildren play an active role in the revitalizing of our cognitive functions. Lack of support increases the potential of decline in health and manifests into various forms of frustrations mainly being unable to perform the physical tasks that were so easy to perform just a few years ago. One of the simplest ways of overcoming frustrations is to meditate and find solace or comfort in our past.

Happiness, Contentment and Enjoyment in acquiring new social skills and interactions are the keys to the fulfilment in retired life.

There are so many cool activities we as elderly citizens can undertake to keep us focused and mentally alert; here are some.

Engaging in artworks, drawing, painting, handicrafts and pottery and many more.

Many people started cultivating arts and crafts of their choice in their later life and became quite successful at it.

If the works of some of the personalities, as referred to below, can induce some inspirational thoughts then their stories and achievements can certainly be a motivational pathway for us to follow. No, not to be as famous as our so-called idols but a pathway to follow to enhance our own self-esteem and balance in life to our longevity.

Mary Delany had a string of bad fortune in her life, she was widowed twice, but she soldiered on and at the age of 68 years, she took up paper cut-outs and made intricate designs of plants and flowers. This kept Mary focused and to march on with a purpose in life. What started as a hobby ended up as collections displayed in the British Museum. She worked until she was 88 years old and displayed some 1700 pieces of fine artwork.

Bill Taylor's story was very interesting yet sad indeed. He was broke and homeless at the age of 85. To pass the time and loneliness he started to draw and display his drawings on the streets of Montgomery in the southern state of Alabama in the USA. He displayed more than 1000 drawings, and his artwork is still displayed even to this day. Imagine being an Afro-American born into slavery, how difficult his life would have been at that time, his efforts and tenacity is really inspiring.

There are many other seniors who started their hobby later in life and achieved some form of success. But, this should not be the point of our narrative, we are not trying to awaken our talents but merely to develop a skill to keep us focused in our quest to live longer, healthier and gracefully. If in this journey fame and fortune become our destiny then it is an added advantage and so be it.

Milestones and stages of our lives:

I have explained earlier the seven stages in our life cycle. For the sake of simplicity, let's consider the following major stages of our life-cycle and milestone experiences. With each milestone, we experience changes within our psychological, physiological and spiritual development along with our physical, cognitive, emotional and other parameters of personal growth. These growth parameters are important from the very early stages of our life cycle as these are the very basic life traits that get etched into our psyche. From **birth to infancy,** we not only go through the growth factor but also start to learn the basic instincts important for our future development such as trust, dependence and self-reliance.

In the next phase of our growing-up, to the **teens and young adulthood,** there are a lot of external interactions which help us with our personal and cognitive development amongst other things such as curiosity factor and self-assessment or realization. This is where we develop our emotional and cultural awareness as to who we are and what our roots are. Cultural and psychological awareness becomes quite strong at this particular stage of our life cycle. **Adulthood** is a very important phase of our life cycle when we reach the peak of our physical and intellectual maturity. This is the age of responsibility, partnerships, and development of various life skills, interactive and social skills and many more which propel us to prepare for tackling day-to-day issues. In the final phase of our life-cycle **"The Ageing"** which officially starts when we are retired and live our lives till we are dead and gone. But to me, the ageing starts at 70 years of age and beyond. To some, this is a very traumatic time full of frustrations and emotional distress. The feeling of being unwanted, useless and dependent can really trigger our self-esteem to a spiralling low.

On the other hand, there are many seniors who consider themselves in a prestigious and eminent position. We have "been there and done that," and by virtue of our life experiences, we still know that we have a lot to contribute to society. Yes, certainly we may not be as computer and technologically savvy as young adults, but that should not be a deterrent; rather our wisdom and ethics cultivated for decades far more compensate for our lack of tech skills.

The ageing in the human life cycle can be demanding from a health and well-being point of view. Anatomical changes linking the physiological disorders faced by many of the seniors can be very challenging. There are several parameters that need to be considered and targeted. The first and foremost challenge that comes to my mind is nutritional requirements in the elderly population along with the health care system and dedication of the caregivers in the area of Health and Age care. Our expectations need to be moderate; we can never expect our physical and mental capacities to function as a young adult and we need to accept that with every year that passes by our various faculties will gradually lose their efficiency and functionality.

So what about nutrition? For those who are self-managed and self-reliant and can still live independently, have a number of options to follow. A balanced meal with appropriate physical exercise can go a long way to Ageing Gracefully. To cope with the anatomical and physiological changes, we need proper nutrition to fuel our finely tuned body and health. The body's need for proteins, amino acids, carbohydrates, fruits, vegetables and nuts, and good fatty acids (mono- and unsaturated) are all essential; additionally, certain vitamins and minerals will enhance the repair of the years of wear and tear and promote a healthy living and longevity.

The World Health Organization (WHO) defines healthy ageing as "the process of developing and maintaining the functional ability that enables wellbeing in older age." The population of aged people (60 years and over) is increasing at an alarming rate. According to 2019 statistics, the number was around 1 billion and is expected to rise to 1.4 billion by 2030 and wait, for it could go up as high as 2.1 billion by 2050. This needs forward planning on behalf of the government and also all of us including current seniors and would-be seniors in time to come. It is obvious that with every stage of our life cycle right from birth to death the ageing cycle is inevitable and therefore, we all must prepare for it while we can, irrespective of our status of dependency or independent living.

Referring to World Health Organization (*Ref: Ageing World Health Organization (WHO) https://www.who.int " Health topics) and view it as a part of their charter on health and wellbeing, the statement reads* "Every person – in every country in the world – should have the opportunity to live a long and healthy life. Yet, the environments in which we live can favour health or be harmful to it. Environments are highly influential on our behaviour and our exposure to health risks (for example, air pollution or violence), our access to services (for example, health and social care) and the opportunities that ageing brings".

Reads and sounds good, but then what can be done about it?

Essentials of ageing gracefully:

The three most basic attributes of life are. physical health, mental health and attitude towards life. These three attributes are the three pillars of ageing gracefully supported by various life responses which give us the wholesome approach to ageing gracefully. If we can maintain and build upon these life responses, then our journey becomes more purposeful.

There are three phases to life once we cross the threshold of being old; be it at 60, 65 or 70 years. Appropriately, our ageing process starts at our retirement.

The first phase starts at the age when we start feeling old. To some, this age may be 70 years and for many others it could be 60 or for some even earlier. This is the transition phase when we start accepting the truth of our ageing process. For some it may not be easy and may lead to mild symptoms of anxiety and depression. The analogy is as we move away from the limelight of the yesteryears, there is a void in our life and the feeling of missing out hits us. Best to overcome these negative feelings as quickly as possible and let inevitability take its course.

Then there is phase two, which is the acceptance phase, now that we have accepted the transition and are moving on with our life as best as we can. The final phase is the execution phase which questions us, ok, now that we have made the transition and accepted changes, what next or what are we going to do about it to make our journey through this transition as pleasant and smooth as possible?

There are many positive life-responses which can lead us through our "ageing gracefully" journey and give us comfort and satisfaction to cope with.

Patience is a virtue: how true is this as we contemplate our retirement we feel sure that we have "Time" on our side. And time is the universal panacea to all healing processes. So, mend all rifts with friends and loved ones and get involved in positive social networking.

Laugh a lot: "You don't stop laughing when you grow old, you grow old when you stop laughing." — George Bernard Shaw

Your best years: are ahead of you, plan and make the best use of those remaining golden years of your life. Keeping this in mind you need to forward-plan your future so that you have plenty of good years to enjoy them.

Planning can be easy if you do not overcrowd your visions for the future; a simplistic approach is a lot better than an elaborate one and see where it takes you. Yes, a slight risk is involved but the romance and the thrill of the experiences, I am sure is more than a fair compensation and worth taking the risk.

First and foremost plan for your health and care by having a complete medical check and assessing the risk factors. Ask your medical doctor to sit down with you and discuss each medical risk factors and map out your plan and alternatives in case of the risk factor weighing heavily against your bucket list. Seek out medical opinions and a simpler alternative to fulfil them. Once you have sorted out the risk factors and your bucket, list then go to the next planning item; your resources and finances. Start saving if you can and scrutinize your finances as you will need a certain nest egg for the rainy days and future days ahead. It may be a bit tricky so you should get some professional help and guidance.

You may also need to downsize and reorganize your estate and valuables to offer that extra bit of flexibility to help you along; you have earned it so go and enjoy.

An important point to consider is your outstanding debts; take care of those at the earliest opportunity to enjoy financial flexibility and independence.

Decluttering is also a tedious task but needs to be done. Some people, especially us older generation are renowned for our ability to hang on to some useless memorabilia. When the time comes to lighten your burden do so; as, along your new journey you are sure to collect a few more.

Have you ever thought of where you would like to live after retirement? Some choose to live near their loved ones, some opt for a more exotic location and some take the drastic action of living in a different country where the living expenses are cheaper than their current living location.

Whatever your preference is, do your homework before you settle on a destination? Importantly, the medical facilities, laws of the land socio-economic environments, culture and customs etc. are issues that would need to be settled upon before any decision is made.

Fitness is very important, no one expects you to be as healthy as a younger middle-aged person, but making regular efforts will certainly bear fruit in your later stage of life when you need your health and fitness the most. But in some cases, many seniors have a good physical fitness level and stamina and if this is you then keep working at it to maintain your fitness level a bit longer. Physical fitness is important because it is the doorway to your health and happiness and lowers your risk levels from secondary ailments. Staying physically fit and active allows you to enjoy more quality time and be productive with your hobbies and social interests.

Try to give up smoking, alcohol and drug abuse, this will give you a cleaner body and mind and could also help you with your sleep and relaxation which are important to lower your lifestyle disease risk factors.

Let us now assume your planning is all done and you are equipped with the required knowledge and information to take on the last phase which is the execution phase.

Live a simplistic life, declutter and keep your body, mind and soul in an active but benevolent state. All else falls into place.

As we read on, we will find how our old age prepares us for life and if the basic mix of the three attributes is right we are well on our way to aging gracefully.

It is not uncommon that societal attitudes toward aging or old age are rather negative, according to Professor of Psychology Susan Whitbourne (University of Massachusetts, Amherst). She comments, "Don't get bogged down in all the hype about aging. Once you start thinking about it, it can drive you mad. There's nothing you can do; the clock is going to tick away."

Old age is not about numbers; we all are eventually going to age and pass on our legacy and wisdom to the next generation. Well and good if they embrace it, if not it's their loss. And conversely, it is our loss as oldies if we only think of the losses or what the old age has taken away from us; think about the gains and what life for the past 60 or 70 years has enriched us with.

Graceful ageing or ageing gracefully is the goal, which entails our physical and mental fitness and our attitude to life and living … after all, we may not have much time to live. It is a futile exercise to harp on our younger, youthful-looking days; the aim is to live out our lives as long as we can and as comfortably as we can. I am not for once saying not to look after ourselves to be more presentable, witty and desirable, but within our means and moderation. Do not play with the priorities; ageing gracefully is trying to live out our lives in comfort, contented and independent as long as we can.

The importance of good restful sleep has been scientifically linked with improvement in cognitive patterns, lowering the risk of cardiovascular complications, stress and depression, obesity and diabetes and many more. However, it is important that if you are suffering from any medical complications mild or severe, you owe it to yourself to seek remedial action by having periodic medical intervention.

Chapter 2

THE AGEING PROCESS

"Ageing is the maturity of life. Those who age well mellow like fine wine—gracefully refined by time."

– Jay Das … 2024

The ageing process is a wonderful phase in life, from the birth of a child to the completion of its life cycle. We must go through an inevitable sequence of events which for many is a wonderful experience and for some can be a daunting and debilitating sequence of circumstances. Aging comes with its own challenges, having to cope with ups and downs and curly situations that life during the aging process could offer. But since it is a reality of life there is no escaping.

There are several theories about ageing that involves hard-core biological, more specifically genetic mediation and also self-programming.

We as organic beings are composed of cellular units as the basic currency of our physical makeup. Our longevity and health conditions are largely dependent on the life cycle of these cellular units; cell divisions, cell multiplications, death and rebirth of cells and genetic programming which pre-determine our health condition. You may have heard that when a child is born, parents are offered Neonatal Screening Tests to determine any genetically predisposed health condition that the parents should be aware of. Some of these conditions may require lifelong management. Just to name a few of these more common conditions.

Blood disorders, Cystic Fibrosis, Inherent Metabolic Disorders, Endocrine Gland disorders, several enzyme insufficiencies and many more.

Although most babies tested do not show any positive screening results, nonetheless, these early detections give valuable information and preparedness for future years. Early medical and clinical intervention can improve severe disabilities and secure a plan for disease and disability management and any future complications.

Elderly people are likely to suffer from multi-disciplinary medical conditions and each has to be identified and treated accordingly and monitored to provide a structured and optimum care regime. For those interested in Genetic Theories and Ageing can do some further reading (*https://www.britannica.com/science/aging-life-process*).

Why do we age, and can we stop the ageing process?

It is a million-dollar question that has been asked in every generation from time immemorial. No satisfactory answers yet; we still have not been able to find the fountain of youth.

Fountain of youth; how interesting, many of you may have heard about it, as I certainly have. However, later in the chapter, we can at least search for it and try to find out the truth behind it.

There are several theories as to why we age.

There are no definitive answers and all theories have their own merits as well as critics.

The Wear and Tear Theory sounds very plausible. As a general rule, most things in Nature have a defined life, our bodies start to wear in our old age resulting in a decline in our bodily functions. The physical deterioration results from the de-naturing, lack of activity and simply wear and tear or damage in the cells, resulting in tissue in-activities which lead to organ rundown and eventually ceases to function. As a general rule, most things in Nature have a defined life, for example, you go to a pharmacy and look up at the medicine counters and you will see that almost all medicines have a "use by' date.

Wear and tear damage could also be due to environmental factors such as pollution, excessive exposure to sunlight and radiation and could also be due to food preservatives, alcohol and drug abuse and build-up of toxicity in the bloodstream as a result of handling hazardous chemicals which ends up in our cells and eventually deposited into the organs, eventually causing organ failure.

In animal kingdoms, just like us new babies are born, they grow up and eventually die. Same in the plant world, there are annuals and perennials. But surprisingly, there are exceptions to the rule. You may have heard that giant sequoia trees of North America have been known to live 2000 years or more. Bowhead whales are also known to live longer, around 200 years. In comparison, a human life can be extended to a maximum of 125 years only; amazing, don't you think? But wait for it, there are trees that have been known to live longer, check out the list below. How does this happen? Marine Biologists have found that Bowhead whales have a mutated gene **ERCC-1** which is involved in repairing the damaged DNA structure and helps protect the whales from several diseases e.g., cancer.

There are many plants that have survived for several centuries continuously and are still living today which makes interesting reading. (*https://www.sciencefocus.com/nature/top-10-oldest-plants-on-the-planet/*). Several examples of these living plant and animal species are presented in the table below.

Name of the Entity	Plant/Animal	Longevity	Reference
Greenland Sharks	Marine **Animal** (Arctic and Nth Atlantic Oceans)	250 years +	1. St. Lawrence Shark Observatory in Canada
Deep sea Tubeworms	Marine Animal Mostly hydrothermal vents	300 years + (up to 1000 years)	2. (*Scientific name Escarpia laminate)*
Black Coral Species	Marine **Animal** coast of Hawaii	4000 years and more	3. *((Scientific name Leiopathes sp.)*
Ocean Quahog	Marine **Animal** coast of Iceland	400 + years	*4. (Scientific name Arctica islandica)*
Immortal Jellyfish	Marine **Animal** Mediterranean Sea	Lives for ever	5. *(Scientific name Turritopsis dohrnii)*
Bristlecone pine	Land Tree White Mountains of California	5000 years	6. *(Scientific name Pinus longaeva)*
Maidenhair tree	Land Tree China and south East Asia	Around 3500 years	7. *(Scientific name Ginkgo biloba)*
Huon pine colony	Land Tree Tasmania Australia	10,000 years	8. (Scientific name
Wollemi Pine	Land Tree Wollemi National Park Australia	200 million old	9. *(Scientific name Araucariaceae family)*
Cycads	South and Central America	280 million years	10. *(Scientific name The Cycadophyta)*

Some of the longevity periods are not continuous for the species, but are a reflection of their ancestors from their fossil records and self-cloning propagation.

References:

1. St. Lawrence Shark Observatory https://geerg.ca " Greenland-shark

2. New Scientist
https://www.newscientist.com " article " 2141387-giant.
3. Conservation International
https://www.conservation.org " blog " newly-discovered..
4. NOAA Fisheries
https://www.fisheries.noaa.gov " science-data " ocean-qu...
5. BBC Earth
https://www.bbcearth.com " news " the-jellyfish-that-ne...
6. USDA
https://www.usda.gov " media " blog " 2011/04/21 " m...
7. Wikipedia
https://en.wikipedia.org " wiki " ginkgo_biloba
8. Ormistonhouse.com.au
https://www.ormistonhouse.com.au " huon-pine
9. NSW National Parks
https://www.nationalparks.nsw.gov.au " plants-and-animals
10. Wisconsin Horticulture – Division of Extension
https://hort.extension.wisc.edu " articles " cycads

Going back to the wear and tear theory, it was first proposed by a German Biologist, Dr. August Weismann, in 1882 and suggested that our ageing process occurs due to progressive decline of our bodily cells and tissues due to environmental conditions such as pollution, exposure to UV radiations, etc., and harmful toxins produced in our body. Dr. Weismann's theory was basically compared with the wear and tear encountered in machine parts due to their overuse. Some of this theory is now being rethought and re-theorised particularly in the area of age-related cell damage and cell self-repair theories. Cells can self-repair with good nutrition and a structured lifestyle. However, there is no denying that over time cells will be damaged and the repair process will take longer even with good nutrition and an improved lifestyle (*Ref: Changes during aging and their association with malnutrition, Geriatrics. 2015; 6(3):78-84*).

One of the fundamental criticisms of the wear and tear theory is that our bodies have a strong ability to repair not only cell damage but also our DNA has repair genes which can offer some protection from DNA damage. In a relatively recent report (*Ioannidou et.al, DNA damage from chronic inflammation to age-related deterioration. Front Genet. 2016; 7:187*), it has been suggested that the ageing process may be partially or completely reversed by simply changing the microenvironment of cells or certain hormonal factors. I leave it up to you to judge for yourself. A good reading reference for those who are interested in further reading is (*www.verywellhealth.com/wear-and-tear-theory-of-aging-2224235*). **The individualism theory of ageing** was put forward by Carl Jung a Swiss psychiatrist (1875-1961), who said, "The afternoon of human life must also have a significance of its own and cannot be merely a pitiful appendage to life's morning. The afternoon of life is just as full of meaning as the morning; only, its meaning and purpose are different...." Carl Jung called the aging process "the afternoon of life" just like the transition of the Sun through the sky, East to Westerly direction, rising in the morning and setting at night. He addressed our adulthood as noon (mid-day) corresponding to our midlife ages while the night was the end of our life stage just like the Sun completes its daily cycle. So, the afternoon was the span of our life from our youth to old age when we are still active and enjoying life. For Jung, the aging process was not one of inescapable decline of body, mind and relevance, but instead a time of progressive refinement and enjoyment. Jung's theory also offers self-assessment as a healthy way to our ageing process from our psychological and spiritual development. Creativity and self-fulfilment can also contribute favourably to a happy and healthy ageing process. Jung's definition of individualism is based on the person's psychological individuality. This is when, according to Jung we acquire the concept of self (individual) and achieve self-realization and develop "ego-centeredness" and individualism. Jung's theory then relates this individualisation with individualised personality which affects our health and well-being and hence may be equated to our longevity. There are several other ageing theories that have been put forward in the past; most of which are extensions of biological and genetic modifications. The basic concept of ageing we need to focus upon are as follows: We are born to go through the ageing process, this is inevitable. Our bodies, both anatomically and psychologically, cannot cope with after a certain age. We are prone to sickness and diseases due to lower immunity as we age which also puts a burden on our ageing process.

Our psychological state of health declines when we are old for a number of reasons primarily due to loneliness, congenital and mental issues.

What is the secret of longevity in the animal kingdom and the plant world? In general, plants live longer than animals because plants use their stem cells which can aid in the regeneration of new cells. The so-called stem cell bio-technology works better for plants than animals and this causes a protective measure against DNA damage. Compared to animals, plants have much slower growth and metabolism and can revert to a state of dormancy if and when required.

Why can't we extend our life beyond our limit of life extension which is normally this side of one hundred; maybe a maximum of 125 or a bit more in very few instances? The average life expectancy of the world population was around 75.6 years (for females) and 70.8 years (for males) according to 2020 statistics; Australia (83.9 years), Hong Kong (85.3 years), Singapore (84.1 years), New Zealand (82.8 years). United Kingdom (81.8 years) rank amongst the highest life expectancy for both sexes, while people in the sub-continent countries like India (70.4 years), Pakistan (67.8 years), Sri Lanka (77.6 years) and Bangladesh (73.6 years) ranked lower. (*Ref:https://www.worldometers.info/demographics/*

life-expectancy/). The answer is complex and yet to be found. There are, however, research reports that appear from time to time for the increase in global life expectancy but currently it seems too farfetched and there is no concrete evidence to even contemplate any positive euphoria. One such report recently appeared in Scientific American (*Ref:https://www.scientificamerican.com/article/humans-could-live-up-to-150-years-new-research-suggests*) about the possible discovery of a new molecule that may prevent age-related diseases and increase life expectancy and wellness (August 1, 2022, The Hebrew University of Jerusalem).

What is the ageing process and when does it start?

In a recent article published in (*Ref: www.msdmanuals.com/en-au/home/older-people%E2%80%99s-health-issues/the-aging-body/overview-of-aging*) by Richard G. Stefanacci (Thomas Jefferson University, Jefferson College of Population; last modified Sep 2022) the author has elegantly described the process of ageing.

According to the author, Aging is a gradual, continuous process of natural change that begins in early adulthood. During early middle age, many bodily functions begin to gradually decline.

Let me add by saying that the ageing process virtually starts since the day we are born. Every day or year that passes by we become that much older and our body prepares us to make subtle changes to cope with getting old, and one fine morning, we wake up and see ourselves self-embracing, accumulative subtle changes, which is called the ageing process. There is no fixed age when we become old, but the general consensus is that 65 years and above is the benchmark. But, having said that, it is highly individual and varies greatly from person to person. Again referring back to Richard G. Stefanacci's article there are three age classifications we can identify in order to answer "when a person does become old".

Chronological age: This is based on a person's true age and reflects their health condition in terms of their normal physical and psychological wear and tear for the age. And it is very likely that the decline in health condition will be in accordance with the normal age and in most normal cases can be predicted.

Biological age: This is referred to as a measure of our physical and mental function. In some of us this age may have some genetic, environmental and socio-economic significance. Some people tend to age sooner and look older for their age while there are some enviable people in our society who can hold their age better and even at the age of 80 look fit and healthy as if they were only 60 years old.

Psychological age: This is very interesting and is gauged by your mental attitude and how one feels. This can go either way; you can be older than you look and have all the attributes of an elderly citizen, or you can be much younger in your looks for your age and behave how you look and feel. For these people, it is very hard to estimate their chronological age and may not require any professional help even when you may qualify for it. So, what do these three ages define and what are the advantages of categorising the aged population according to these three age groups? First part of the question, is there any real benefit?

Chronological age is your real age, every year that passes by you add on to your chronological age irrespective of how you look and feel.

There is not a great deal of difference between our biological age and our psychological age. Biological age relates to our anatomical attributes. Some people age quickly and may look 10 years older than their chronological age due to several reasons for example their socio-economic stress situation which may reflect on their anatomy, e.g., skin starts to wrinkle, abnormality in their skeletomuscular frame-work causing a stooping gait, etc.

Physiological age tends to probe more into the effect of our genetic dispositions.

Some studies have indicated that our "mental age" could have some influence on our longevity. I know by introducing the "mental age" qualification, we are introducing another ageing process; don't be confused as for the sake of simplicity, we can equate mental age to psychological age. In the findings of a study (*Ref: www.kfucoidan.com/health/202202/*), it has been reported that people with a higher mental age (psychological age) than their chronological age have a higher risk of death. People with a lower psychological age look forward to a brighter future and greater longevity.

This is irrespective of your social and demographic factors.

It is therefore very important to be fit and young and have a positive attitude to life in order to boost your life span and age gracefully.

Anatomically, the ageing process involves several changes in our organs and the systems within our body.

Let us look at age-related changes in a more detailed but generalised way for easy understanding. The first visible sign under the normal ageing process is the change in our appearance, our hair is greying and we may start shedding hair strands in clumps, we often lose our upright posture from our youthful years, and our tooth decay may also show up and our skin anatomy undergoes marked changes.

Folks, do not despair as this is the law of Nature and eventually, we become one with Nature.

Skin is our largest external organ which practically covers the entire body. Our skin has several layers, the outermost layer, the Epidermis begins to thin out due to the deterioration in the cellular integrity. The outermost skin layer sheds around 2g of dead cells every day. In young adults, the lost skin cells are replenished at a much faster rate than in an elderly person which exacerbates thinning in the skin structure.

The appearance of sagging skin and wrinkles are also very common signs of ageing skin which are usually caused by the dryness of the skin, lack of proteins (specially elastin), nutrients, e.g., collagen and fatty acids from the dermis and the subcutaneous layers, both of which are sub-epidermis layers of our skin. Age-related dryness of the skin is often due to a decline in the activities of the sweat glands and oil glands, both located in the epidermis and the dermis layer. This results in the outermost layer of our skin, the epidermis not getting enough moisture and lubrication, giving it a dry and rough appearance. Lack of moisture also causes loss in the body's temperature control. The sweat glands provide the outer layer of our skin with sweat (moisture) which then evaporates causing a cooling effect. So, we can say it is like an internal Air-conditioning system which with aging becomes inefficient. The further implication of this is that our skin can damage easily with minor cracks and bruising likely to appear that takes much longer to mend.

There are several non-anatomical reasons for skin damage in the elderly such as the effects of medication (e.g. topical application of steroids), effect of excess UV radiation, environmental pollution, and often overlooked effects of the harsh and corrosive chemicals from the cosmetic application on the skin.

Our skin, young or aged is very sensitive and can damage easily but it is quite resilient too and heals quickly thanks to the process of rejuvenation of the dead cells, although faster in younger than in older skin.

Lack of natural pigmentation and natural protective effects of the ageing skin can cause irreversible damage. This has a flow on detrimental effect on temperature regulation, vitamin D synthesis, impaired new cell growth, storage and synthesis of essential bio-chemicals, e.g., fatty acids, proteins, collagen and essentially the integrity of blood vessels and capillaries which are located under the bottom layer of the dermis. This will eventually lead to higher stress levels on the aged skin causing visible age or liver spots, itch and eczema, fragile blood vessels, causing to bruise easily and haemorrhage.

What changes are likely to take place as we start ageing?

Besides our appearance, greying hair and sagging and wrinkled skin there are several anatomical and physiological changes that prepare us for our senior years. Deterioration in the Anatomical constitution disrupts and weakens our Physiological functions. Let's start with simple issues as we will later concentrate on the larger and more serious anatomical and physiological factors that will affect our old age.

Sensory changes: With ageing our sensory perceptions change significantly; hearing, sight, taste, smell and touch are the sensory parameters that connect older people to the outside world and also connect them socially. Impairment in any of the sensory faculties could cause low esteem, stress, depression and other forms of mental anguish which later may manifest in some form of major problem for the sufferer to deal with.

Sensory changes would mainly be concerned with a gradual decline in sight and hearing senses which is quite common in seniors of advanced age. These can be rectified to a certain degree by medical intervention. Certain supplementary aspects may also help such as administering Vitamin A, Beta-carotene and a diet rich in carrots, leafy vegetables and yellow pumpkins.

Hearing loss can be compensated for by using hearing aids.

Sensory perceptions and messages are taken to the brain via the sensory nerves and return to the sensory organs concerned, e.g., finger touch, smell through the nose and taste through the taste buds in the mouth. The stronger the return message or command from the brain the stronger the feeling or the senses. The brain sends signals via the motor nerves to the peripheral nerve system for the activation of the sensory organs.

Neurotransmitters are the actual biochemical molecules that transmit and or carry messages from neurons to and from the brain for the actual messages and commands to be relayed to the appropriate section of the peripheral nerve system.

There are many bio-chemical neurotransmitters in our body and almost 100 have been identified of which the common neurotransmitters are glutamate, acetylcholine, glycine, norepinephrine etc. Acetylcholine is well known and studied neurotransmitter that plays an essential role in muscle movement, memory function, power of thinking, and general activity of the brain; (*Ref: Curr Opin Neurobiol. 2006 Dec; 16(6):710-5. This being highly studied many other references are available e.g. Neurochem. 2017 Aug; 142 Suppl 2(Suppl 2):111-121*).

It has been reported that a low level of acetylcholine is associated with learning difficulties, memory loss and decline in brain function as is in the cases of dementia and Alzheimer's disease (*Ref: Age Ageing. 2006 Jul;35(4):336-8*).

Supplementary intake of an individual or a combination of neurotransmitters can assist in several health benefits. Intake of Lecithin supplementation can improve the choline and acetylcholine levels in the body.

Other changes of concern we need to be aware of as a part of aging are:

A feeling of lethargy and literally slowing down: Our body will feel tired, and run down, especially in the mornings during wake-up time when stiffness and aches and pains will be quite normal.

This is due to lack of physical activities and slowing down of the brain receiving and sending signals to our muscles and other sensory organs that control our movements.

Dental hygiene will be affected: Tooth decay and gingivitis may happen with bacterial infections. Regular trips to the dentist and increased dental hygiene and care may be required.

Bruises will happen more often: This is a very common occurrence in our old age as our skin becomes thinner and the integrity of our blood vessels, particularly the capillary blood vessels becomes weak and fragile and are prone to bleeding and therefore bruise easily.

Stooping gait: It is not uncommon for many of us to lose a noticeable height and posture as we age. It has been estimated that we could lose around 1.5 cm every 10 years starting at the age 70 years (from a report published by the Medical University of South Carolina). This is a part of, shall we say, depreciation of our Skeletomuscular system with age.

Other common changes are hormonal imbalance or insufficiencies which control our sexual activities, weight management, and general attitude to life, when pessimism takes over, are quite distinctly noticeable.

I am just generalizing as this could happen but not necessarily going to happen. There are many senior citizens who live and enjoy every aspect of their senior years, they have a special attitude to life which we all could learn from.

Sarcopenia is an old age disease that affect elderly people. Although it affects seniors in the age group 65 years and above, when behavioural and lifestyle issues contribute to the decline in the protein mass and their frame.

It is sometimes Adults aged 30 to 40 years who may also start losing muscle mass and strength.

Sarcopenia is also known as muscle wasting disease and can be a debilitating condition in elderly people. In some seniors with this condition participation in simple daily activities can be difficult as the weakness in muscles takes over and there is progressive loss in muscle strength.

Prognosis can be very hurtful for the sufferers; they may lose their daily movement and independence and may need long-term or lifelong care.

What are the simple symptoms and risks of this disease? The control of muscle movements gets progressively weaker.

Progressively slowing of the walking pace.

Difficulty in simple chores such as lifting a glass of water to drink.

Loss of steadiness or balance causing occasional fall.

The risk of fractures from falls increases.

Requirement of care and management of the condition increases.

Obesity and inactivity can increase muscle weakness.

Malnutrition, diabetes, and certain autoimmune diseases e.g. rheumatoid arthritis and cancer are risk factors that can progress the disease at a faster rate.

Muscle wasting disease can affect both male and female seniors and unfortunately, medical intervention in the form of patient care is needed.

Protein-enriched dietary regimen and well-structured physical activity are the only options to help increase muscle mass.

Spirituality and psychology of the ageing process:

Spirituality is the feeling we are born with. Many of us nurture this inner feeling as we grow in life. Our environment, our parents' influence and the ethnicity of our upbringing help us develop this inner quality that stays with us till the end of our life cycle.

After the early stages of initiation, more often it becomes a self-cultivated realization that guides these inner feelings and provides us with peace and strength during our dark days. Spirituality may not have any strong binding with religion, it may just be a practice in the form of yoga and pranayama which are ancient forms of practices to calm our body and control our mind so that we stay focused in life and events ahead. Meditation is an excellent way and relates to spirituality without any physical effort. It is a good way of staying focused in our advancing years.

There is a very intimate bonding between spirituality and psychology.

Psychology is derived from the Greek words "Psyche" and "Logos". The union between mind and soul.

Therefore, the bonding of Spirituality–Psychology becomes an essential tool to understand ourselves from a mind and soul-searching point of view. It makes the search more complete and meaningful.

But why is this bonding important as we age? By combining the two, we can get answers to the questions we have within ourselves.

What is the Purpose of our life?
What is happiness and peace?
What are our responsibilities and how can we handle them?
What makes us humans?

If we all look in-depth into these questions, we will soon find the relationship between Spirituality–Psychology. The answer lies within our inner vaults; we just have to unlock it.

How does this, then help us with our health issues in our old age?

Mind and Soul have a strong link with our physical body. There is a saying that "A healthy Body harbours a healthy Mind". There is a strong belief that our physical body reacts positively to good environment such as good news, good company and good emotions etc. This has now been tested scientifically and in most cases proven positive.

In several detailed review-based studies it was reported that psychological health and cardiovascular disease (CVD) are well connected (*Ref: Circulation Vol. 143, No. 10 Psychological Health, Well-Being, and the Mind-Heart-Body Connection: A Scientific Statement from the American Heart Association*).

If we can dissect our physical body according to its main bodily functions, we can arrive at certain discussion points about Brain (body computer), digestive system (body food processing source) and heart (body life stream).

Our Brain controlling our central nervous system CNS, is like the command centre for the body works and is connected to our spinal cord the backbone of our body that has myriads of functions such as producing bone marrow where the red blood cells are manufactured.

Brain anatomy is quite complex, but keeping it simple our brain receives and gives signals that are relayed to our muscle structure for Body Organ Movements. In older people due to a gradual decline in brain activity, the movements and joint activities are slower than in younger adults. Also, the power of thinking and analysing (cognitive and mental activities) can be gradually impaired.

Our digestive system is the food processing source and supplier for the body's nutritional needs. Food that we eat is converted into basic absorbable units for our body to utilise. If our digestive system is not functioning optimally then our body, more appropriately body cells, cannot process the absorbable food units into energy and our body can starve and become weak and eventually perish. Again, our digestive system is quite complex with the involvement of several individual organs working together.

Our heart is the centre of the body co-ordinating the traffic flow and organising the supply chain to be correctly delivered to the right organ and bringing back the unwanted material for processing or elimination. The heart is responsible for the blood circulation. It is the life-giving delivery system delivering oxygen and nutrients into the required tissues and brain so that none of the organs starve but they keep functioning to sustain life. The heart is also called the ticker because like clockwork it keeps ticking on pumping blood throughout our body and once the ticker stops it signals the end of our life cycle. A healthy heart is a healthy body.

Our heart is the central organ of our cardiovascular system (CVS).

With ageing the effectiveness of the heart function diminishes resulting in the weakness in many of our organ functions.

Now, the big question is how to maintain and improve our body functions when we are ageing and therefore **Age Gracefully**.

The old age remedy, Nature. Our ancestors were at one with nature and took Mother Nature's generous bounty. Today we are going back to the same principles backed by science.

Nature and the natural environment also have a strong positive connection with good health and well-being (*Ref: Spending at least*

120 minutes a week in nature is associated with good health and well-being. Sci Rep 9, 7730 (2019).

Nature has a calming effect on our mind and body. This in effect can trigger a positive vibe in many bodily functions, especially, in our aged population. It is well known and well researched that a calm body has the following physiological effects. It lowers blood pressure, relieves stress, improves circulation and eases symptoms of mental health anxiety and depression.

In 2012, the American College of Rheumatology Recommended the Use of Non-pharmacologic and Pharmacologic Therapies in Osteoarthritis (OA) of the Hand, Hip, and Knees. The guidelines conditionally recommend tai chi, along with other non-drug approaches such as manual and thermal therapies, self-management programs, and walking aids, for managing knee OA (*Arthritis Care and Research Vol. 64, No. 4, April 2012, pp 465– 474*).

Further research reports in 2016 proved this point (Ref: www.nccih.nih.gov/health/providers/digest/mind-and-body-practices-for-older-adults-science).

Mild forms of Yoga and Tai-chi exercises are less invasive and have proved to be good and popular among older citizens. The effects of meditation are also well studied and researched (Mayo Clinic report).

The above-referenced article also discusses the positive benefits of yoga, tai-chi and other mild forms of exercise for cognitive decline, reduction in the rate of occurrence of falls in elderly citizens and poor balance which are quite common old age health issues.

Activities undertaken outdoors in the Nature increase the production of our feel-good hormones "Endorphins", which also act as neurotransmitters that improve our feel good moods, relieve pain, stress and tension and also increase our feeling and sense of well-being and wellness.

Relaxing outdoors, playing scrabble, working out cross-word puzzles social interactions can be the conduit between the healthy aging process and senior citizens.

There have been many interesting research-based findings co-relating to outdoor activities and life satisfaction among the elderly. Results satisfactorily supported a higher life satisfaction value.

The Pyramid of Life, trilogy of our existence,

(Body Mind and Soul)

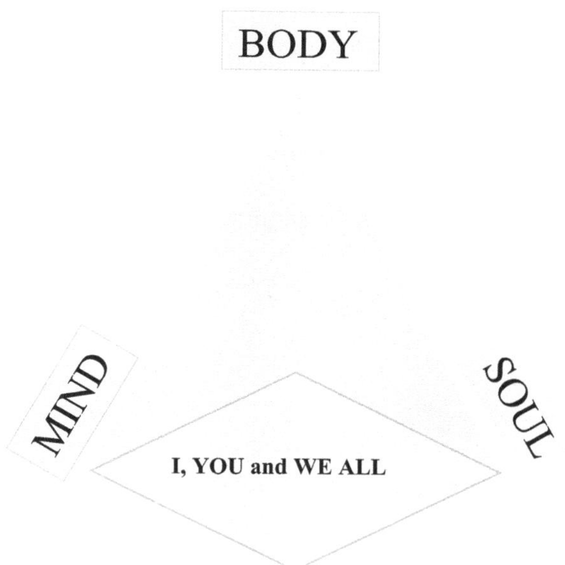

Effect of ageing process on anatomy and physiology:

The ageing process is invariably associated with declining health characterized by degeneration in body organ system. Deterioration in the health of one or several organs resulting in systemic failures could affect the Physiological functionality.

Some individuals with a stronger constitution may be able to cope with the deteriorating organ or organ system with age and prolong the degeneration temporarily and thus, buy more time to prepare for and face the inevitable physiological challenges and functional decline.

Biological sequence of ageing:

It is a sequential process whereby birth to death could be explained from a biological science point of view.

From childbirth (infant) to various stages of growth, ageing can be exemplified by way of ascending the ladder. After birth, the infant goes through several stages of age and developmental phases.

The chart below is a good representation of our life cycle.

Nine Biological stages of our life-cycle

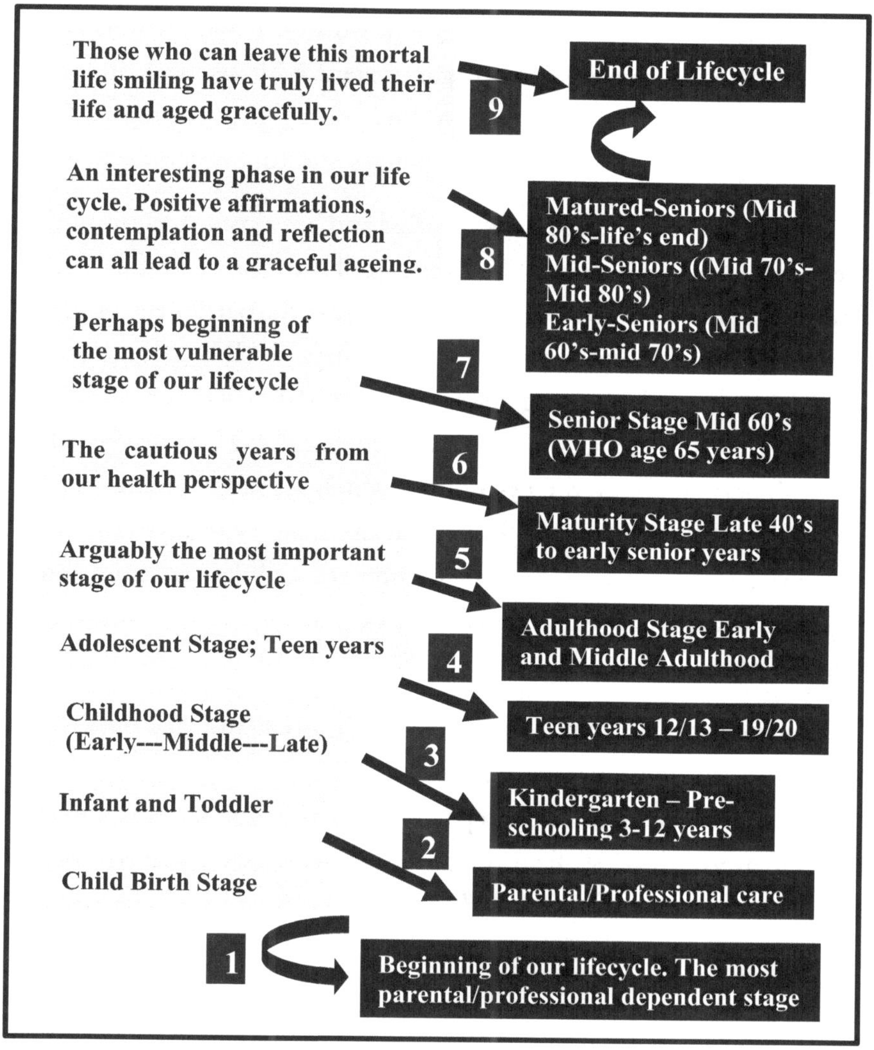

Effect of ageing process on anatomy and physiology:

The ageing process is invariably associated with declining health, characterized by degeneration in the body organ systems. Deterioration in the health of one or several organs resulting in systemic failures could affect the Physiological functionality.

Some individuals with a stronger constitution may be able to cope with the deteriorating organ or organ system with age and prolong the degeneration temporarily. This may buy more time to prepare for the inevitable and face physiological challenges and functional decline.

The structure of a human cell is varied and has a complex composition. The diagram below is a simplified version of our cell structure. There are many individual entities within our cells that are the participants in cellular activities. One of the primary cellular activities is cell division. A tired or ageing cell grows larger and more fragile and has weaker cell division activity. They start to accumulate waste material, e.g., decomposed fatty material, particularly in the Lysosomes, which act as a waste management unit within the cell structure. Lysosome also helps with digestion of food particles, bacteria and viruses which enter the cellular structure through circulation. Christian René de Duve a Belgian biologist, was awarded a shared Nobel Prize in

Physiology (Medicine) in 1974. With tired and ageing cells, the decline in cell division and accumulation of wastes greatly hinders the oxygen and nutrient-carrying capacity. This also hinders waste material, such as carbon dioxide, from being eliminated. The collective negative effects of this can manifest in old age diseases, mainly cellular and tissue dysfunction and a decline in organ activity.

A Simplified diagram of Cellular Structure

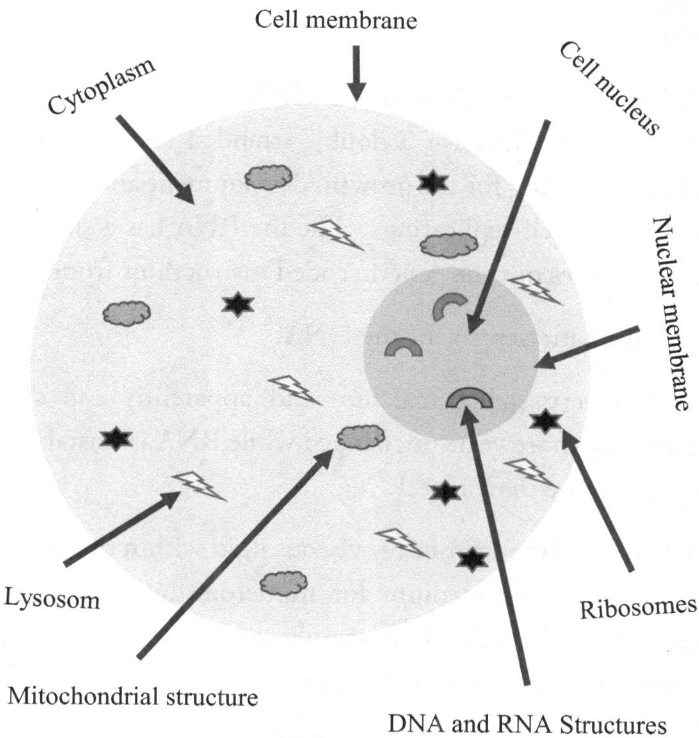

Some of the components of the cellular structure, also called the **Organelles** are Lysosomes, Ribosomes, Mitochondrial structure, cell nucleus, etc., as labelled in the diagram. There are several others not referred to in the diagram, but none the less, they are also important components of the cellular structure.

Cell Nucleus: The cell nucleus is the head office or the administration centre of our cells where most of the genetic material is held.

Most cells have a single nucleus, but exceptions are the red blood cells that have none and the skeletal tissue cells in many cases have two. The cell nucleus is protected by the nuclear membrane which encapsulates the cell nucleus.

DNA (Deoxyribonucleic acid) and RNA (Ribonucleic Acid): Both are genetic materials, DNA is a double-stranded helix structure which contains genetic coding for the growth, development and functioning of all organisms. It is self-replicating, while the RNA has a single-stranded structure and carries out the genetic coded instructions from the DNA.

RNA is like a messenger for the DNA.

DNA is a very stable structure and apparently can survive for hundreds or even more years unchanged while RNA is unstable and may not survive for more than a week.

Cytoplasm: It is the clear heavy viscous fluid within the cell including the nucleus and is the medium for numerous biochemical reactions happening within the cells. It is mainly water and salts and contains enzymes, various organic molecules and various other cellular entities.

Ribosomes: These are like chemical factories which synthesise specific protein molecules from instructions given by the DNA transcripted RNA. These ribosomes are an essential part of all living cells and are abundant in most living cells.

Lysosomes: Lysosomes are integrated cell entity or organelles that are biochemical entities inside a cellular structure that have several specific functions. Lysosomes are involved in cellular processes of breaking down proteins, carbohydrates, fats and lipids, and various other bio-molecules, that need to be broken down in the cells. They also are needed may to destroy the invasion of viruses and bacteria in our cellular structure. These lysosomes are an integral part of our cell structure.

Mitochondria: These are well-organised and defined self-contained entities within our cells where a number of important biochemical activities are continuously taking place. Our mitochondrial structure is a very important organelle within our cellular structure as it produces energy molecules (ATP) that are the food for all our cells and cellular activities. It drives our organs to perform the most basic life-sustaining processes without which we cannot survive. Every cell in every living organism (bacteria, parasites, fungi and all others) has mitochondria in its cellular structure. Some organs have more mitochondria in their cell compared to certain other organs. This increased number is directly related to the energy needs for that particular organ to sustain life; e.g., our heart contains the highest number of mitochondria estimated to be around 5000 mitochondria in each cardiac muscle cell. It is estimated that there are around 2 billion cardiac muscle (heart muscle) cells which means there are around 10 trillion mitochondrial structures in our heart, give or take a few billion; an astronomical number! Why do we have so many mitochondrial structures in our heart? Because they need a lot of energy to keep our heart functioning and blood pumping.

Our genes, chromosomes, DNA and RNA

The topic above is an important aspect of our life cycle. We are born with a set of genetically coded instructions which pre-determines and predisposes a lot of our general characteristics. This could mean the possibility of future development of one, or several disease conditions and/ or inherited traits, inborn errors of our metabolism. Our genes can also influence and characterise our behavioural patterns mental and or psychological issues and many of the physiological parameters which influence our lifecycle. It must also be mentioned that the degree of variance in characteristics may be determined largely by the existing circumstances. With present-day advancements in health science, medicine and lifestyle, severe impairments due to genetic predisposition can be eased remarkably.

Our Genes: It is suggested that our genes are passed on from one generation to the next, parents to off-springs, and is like a family inheritance. Scientifically, it is a biological information coded into our DNA which determines our trait. We have around 20,000-25,000 different genes; 50% of these are inherited from our biological father and the other half from our biological mother. Our DNA are the molecules which carry the genetic information and are a part of chromosomes which are mainly found in the nucleus of our cell, some are located in the mitochondrial structure of each cell where they are entrusted to produce energy.

Chromosomes: There are 23 pairs of chromosomes (46 individuals) in each cellular nucleus, each of these pairs are inherited from our biological parents. Chromosomes are long threaded structures with one molecule of DNA and protein that make up one molecule of the chromosome. They come in different sizes depending on the number of genes, the DNA information, coding and the size of the protein molecules. The amount of genetic information contained in the chromosome also determines its size. Genes in each of the chromosomes are arranged in a very particular sequence and each gene is specifically positioned in a particular location in the threaded chromosome structure. The connection between our DNA, Genes and Chromosomes is shown in the following diagram;

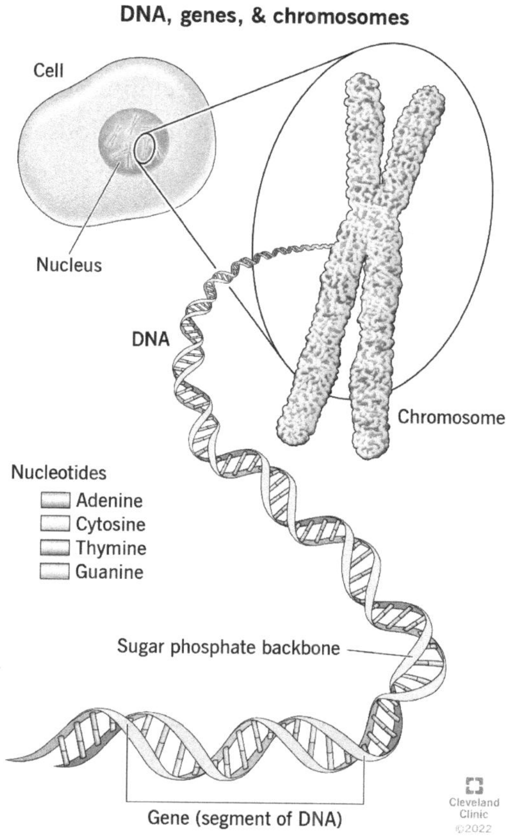

(Gratefully Referenced: DNA, Genes and Chromosomes Overview Cleveland Clinic

(*Ref: www.my.clevelandclinic.org/health/body/23064-dna-genes--chromosomes*).

We know that DNA issues instructions to the RNA which carries out those instructions diligently unless there is some genetic impairment somewhere in the cellular system. So, how does RNA perform its tasks, and also, what is the sequence of events before even DNA issues the instructions? Remember all this is initiated inside the cell nucleus. The end product is specific functional protein molecules which take part in various functions, in the entire cellular structure of our body, such as repair and maintenance, growth and development, participate in the body's defence mechanism, biosynthesis of various biochemicals and many other functions required daily for the body's tissues and organs.

Under normal health, our body uses the same amount of protein that is available within our biological system, however, excess demand arises at the time of our ill health, surgical procedures e.g., convalescing patients, pregnancy and breastfeeding situations. Additional demands also arise after training and gym sessions, athletics and other strenuous workloads.

Basically, there are 3 steps from DNA instructions to Protein synthesis and these are:

Step 1: Our DNA has all the information encoded about us, our traits, our physical attributes even to the extent of the colour of our eyes and all the information that is required for the present and our future growth and development, and also for our survival and future propagation. We can call it a blue print for our makeup not just for now but also for the future.

So, step one simply requires the DNA Genetic decoding of the required message.

Step 2: The decoded message is then picked up by the RNA; to be more precise by the mRNA which is the messenger RNA.

Step 3: In the final step the mRNA is decoded to bio-synthesize the required protein molecules.

This procedure in molecular biology is termed "Dogma" which simply enunciates the 3 fundamental steps of protein synthesis. The 3 steps appear to be simple biological steps but are far more complex and require the involvement of the sequencing of several amino acids to be in unique structural configurations to synthesize the specific protein.

Any changes or impairment in our genes can lead to various genetic and hereditary diseases; see below the sub-category "Genetic Predisposition".

Simple steps in DNA decoding

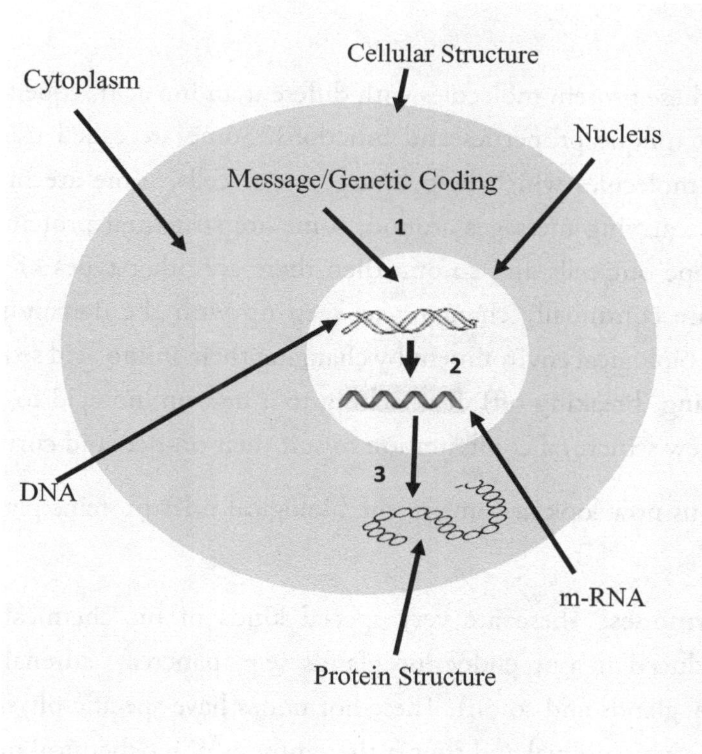

Proteins, as we know, are a significant part of our diet, (10-35%) irrespective of the biological protein synthesis. This intake of protein is very important for supplementing our daily quota of energy requirements.

But, there is another side to proteins which play a very important role in our biochemical makeup. There are numerous kinds of proteins which differ in shape, size and chemical structure and composition. Fundamentally, proteins are composed of many single units called amino acids. These amino acids link with each other in varying configurations to construct larger protein molecules. There are around 20 known amino acids, so you can imagine the numerous protein molecules that can be constructed by various combinations of amino acids linking with each other.

All these protein molecules with different amino acid sequences have different unique properties and functions. Some are called transporter protein molecules which help transport our cells, some are messenger proteins carrying messages around, some are structural proteins which help shape our cells and so on. Then there are other types of proteins which are continually changing to keep up with the demands of our internal biological environment by changing their amino acid sequencing by splicing (breaking off) or attaching to a new amino acid to give it a whole new structural configuration to suit their on-demand current role.

Let us now look at some of the biological roles proteins play in our body.

Hormones: These are very special kinds of bio-chemicals which are produced in our endocrine glands (e.g. pancreas, adrenal glands, pituitary glands and so on). These hormones have specific physiological activities which signal and trigger the synthesis of biochemical molecules which activate various pathways to solve specific needs of our body. For example, we all are familiar with insulin which is excreted by the pancreas and in times of need, when there is an excess of glucose circulating in our blood, insulin is deployed to counteract that and avoid the overloading of glucose in the blood and our cells.

Enzymes: Enzymes can be designated as large highly specialized types of protein molecules which have very specific functions in the body. These are biological catalysts which also contain specific amino acids and speed up biochemical reactions.

There are many examples of various enzyme systems at work in our body and one of the most common examples is the digestive enzyme e.g., Amylase which is a salivary enzyme (mouth, from the salivery gland) that starts the digestive processes in our mouth.

Its specific action is to start the digestive action of carbohydrates in our diet. Another very common enzyme is pepsin which is a stomach enzyme that works on protein digestion (meat, fish, etc.) and converts them into amino acids. Without pepsin, which is secreted in our stomach, our digestive system would not be able to digest proteins, fats and oils.

Antibodies: Let's now move on to our body's defence mechanism and look at the contribution protein makes. When our body is invaded by some infection and our immunity is low, a certain type of proteins swings into action. Antibodies are protein molecules which circulate in our circulatory system. Their job is to find, recognize and neutralize the effects of any foreign bodies that may have penetrated our immune system. Without antibodies the biological foreign bodies e.g., bacterial infection, harmful pollutants, viruses, fungal infections and many other toxins can be very harmful and may cause severe infection in our body. Sometimes, a metabolite or an unwanted fragment of a medicinal product and preservatives from our food supply chain can cause damage to our system and needs to be neutralized by the antibodies in our immune system.

Sometimes there are other ingredients which can step in and boost our immune system; such as, vitamin C which is a good antioxidant and helps mop up the reactive oxygen toxic species (ROTS) also known as reactive oxygen species (ROS) which are formed inside our body and circulates in the bloodstream. These are highly reactive and toxic and are formed, by the decomposition of molecular oxygen, during cellular respiration.

Structural protein: The function of these protein molecules is to provide structural support to our body parts. For example, Collagen and Elastin are the two major proteins which provide support for our skin, bones and connective tissues. Another example is Keratin which provides structural support to our skin, hair and nails. Structural proteins are very important as they do support our movements by strengthening our connective tissues which hold the joints in place, therefore, facilitating our movement and posture.

We have now looked at several important biological functions of proteins, now the question is how different protein structures are constructed to participate in various biological processes. The answer is quite complex but the processes are quite smooth. All proteins that take part in our biological processes are pre-coded genetically. Our genes which are segments of our DNA carry the precoded instructions to bio-synthesize proteins by sequencing together different amino acids and combining them into unique proteins to carry out specific biological tasks. This bio-synthesis happens in three steps as discussed above.

After the DNA decoded message is off-loaded to the messenger RNA (mRNA) the decoded message is then carried out of the nucleus to the cytoplasm which is the viscous fluid encasing the cells. From there on the message is carried on to the transfer RNA (tRNA) which actually constructs the specific protein structure by assembling individual amino acids in a sequence.

Genetic predisposition

Genetic predisposition is a term used in the case of someone who is very likely to be affected with a disease or a condition contributed by the person's genetic encoding. This DNA-coded gene is the predisposition of a particular trait and is located in the chromosomes. Each cell in our body has DNA-encoded gene that pre-empts the behavioural trait and the physical appearance of the person.

Chromosomes, genes and DNA determine the blue-print of the physical and psychological characteristics and instruct the body in their specific protein synthesis which gives us unique features and characteristics.

A genetic predisposition can be determined by conducting specific genetic tests to ascertain the risk of a particular disease which may help take precautions and plan ahead to manage and meet challenges to stay healthy.

There is a range of medically diagnosed health conditions that can simply be managed by lifestyle changes and or taking regular medication as a part of the management program or at worse medical intervention such as surgery.

There are many common diseases that fall under the category of predisposed medical condition affected by genetic transmission from parents to off-springs, which if managed well can lead to a satisfying future and healthy ageing.

There are 4 important aspects to management

1. Medical Diagnosis by way of specific genetic tests
2. Counselling and care assessment (if required)
3. Treatment regimen
4. And periodic medical assessment

There are many diseases caused by rare genetic, inherited (or both) disorders that occur due to defective enzyme (or enzymes) that affect the metabolic pathways of protein, fat, and carbohydrate resulting in the Inborn Error of Metabolism (IEM). Such biochemical insufficiencies lead to medical complications and rare genetic diseases which manifest as organ and systemic impairment. This rare genetic condition can appear at childbirth and progress into young adulthood; some even cause permanent disability and often death.

Planned management of sufferers with IEM is very challenging; with no simple cure, and with most there are no cures at all, the disease progresses to an ultimate disability and very often death. It is rare that sufferers reach adulthood or midlife. The available options is counselling and as best possible care assessment and facilitation. The prognosis of such disease is poor and uncertain.

Among the most common diseases of the IEM that most of us have heard of are; Phenylketonuria (PKU), Phenylketonuria (PKU) is diagnosed from infancy by noticing a strong odour of an amino acid Phenylalanine (PHE) in the urine, sweat and breath. It also appears in blood in significant quantities, as a result of mutation of the gene PAH, which due to mutation, is unable to send instructions for the enzyme Phenylalanine hydroxylase to be synthesised for the processing of phenylalanine (PHE). As a result, there is a significantly increased level of the amino acid in the bloodstream that saturate tissues and organs.

PKU is a lifelong disease or a serious medical condition and if managed properly may prolong life span.

Dietary considerations are very important in the management of the disease. All intake, dietary or otherwise e.g. food intake, supplements, medication, and liquid intakes, must be meticulously screened for PHE or its metabolites such that there is no build-up or overloading of PHE in the bloodstream. Also, a protein diet of nuts, legumes, soy, etc. must be avoided or a minimum intake as suggested by a professional dietician must be considered. Fruit juices or drinks with the artificial sweetener Aspartame must be avoided.

If this disease is left untreated or undiagnosed then the possibility of severe brain damage and intellectual disability is noticed very early in the life of an infant. Neurological disabilities e.g. seizures, and tremors also appear as regular occurrences, followed by marked psychological traits appear as inadequate social behaviours, emotional problems and several health issues begin to develop.

What is the difference between genetic and hereditary pre-dispositions?

All hereditary diseases are genetic in nature where gene mutation is the main cause of the disease. Hereditary diseases are passed on to the next generation.

In contrast, genetic disease may or may not be hereditary but involves a gene-mutation.

Some common genetic disorders (https://www.healthdirect.gov.au/genetic-disorders)

Examples of certain genetic disorders you may have come across are, Albinism: Albinism is a group of genetic conditions affecting the pigmentation of hair, skin and eyes.

Angelman syndrome: It is a rare syndrome causing physical and intellectual disabilities.

Ankylosing spondylitis: a special kind of arthritic condition affecting the spine Apert syndrome: It is also quite rare, with pressure from the brain causing a shape disfiguration of the skull. It can also cause the finger and toe bones to fuse.

Congenital adrenal hyperplasia: This is a group of genetic disorders where the adrenal glands malfunction affecting a child's normal growth and development including genitals.

Other common examples of diseases from gene mutation are Haemophilia, Cystic Fibrosis, Sickle Cell Anaemia, Hemochromatosis, etc. The table refers to some common diseases of genetic mutation that you may have heard of.

Table: Some common diseases of the genetic mutation.

Diseases of gene mutation	**Disease (What is it?)**	**Genetic cause/mutation**
Haemophilia	A bleeding disorder caused by gene mutation	Mutation of the gene which regulated the clotting factor
Cystic Fibrosis	Irreversible damage, over a period of time, to the digestive and respiratory systems due to the build-up of sticky viscous mucus to the organ linings e.g. Lungs, Liver, Intestines etc.	Gene mutation in the gene "cystic fibrosis transmembrane conductance regulator" CFTR which regulates the movement of water and electrolytes from the cells.
Huntington's disease	Huntington's disease of the brain cells brought on by a genetic disorder. It has a very debilitating effect on brain function and coordination resulting in a gradual decline in cognitive and movement functions. It is an incurable disease but with proper disease management sufferers can be helped.	It is an inherited condition caused by the gene mutation of the HTT gene which is responsible for the synthesis of a protein known as Huntingtin which helps with the functioning of our neurons (brain cells). HTT mutation causes an impairment of Huntingtin manufacture.

Haemo-chromatosis	This is a disease of excess build-up of iron in the body particularly skin, heart, liver and several endocrine glands (e.g., pancreas, pituitary), and joints which causes toxicity. This leads to organ dysfunction and even failure and the body can shut down bit by bit and eventually die.	The cause of Hemo-Chromatosis is due to gene mutation of the gene HFE which regulates the iron absorption in our body. The overloading of iron gets stored in various organs and in due time if the disease is not managed effectively then Organ failure takes place.
Down Syndrome	The extra set of chromosome 47 instead of 46 in each cell causes an abnormality in the development of the brain functions, growth retardation and some appearance changes.	It is a genetic disorder caused by an extra copy of chromosome 21 (normally a baby is born with 46 chromosomes)

Simplified map of Genetic Pre-disposition:

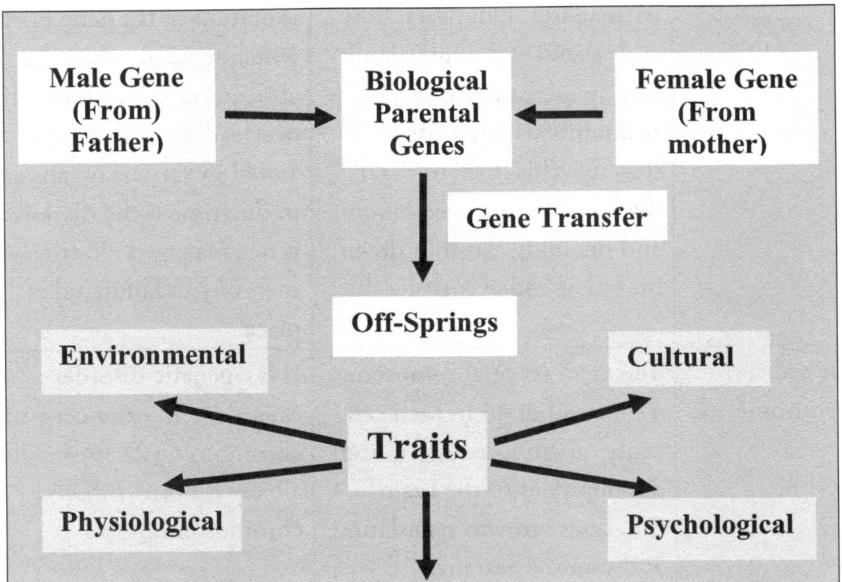

A few conditions related to Genetic Pre-disposition)

- Inborn error of metabolism (due to mutation of specific enzyme)
- Physical appearance, eye, hair colour; gene transfer
- Birth defects and abnormalities; genetic issues, medical, drug and alcohol abuse etc. during pregnancy.
- Albinism; variants in several genes.
- Common today's health issues e.g. diabetes, obesity, cancer, cardiovascular etc.; due to environmental and minor genetic indisposition.
- Mental issues; genetic and lifestyle

A CLEANER AND HEALTHY LIFESTYLE CAN IMPROVE OUR CHANCES OF EASING SOME OF THE PREDISPOSED HEALTH CONDITIONS, ALTHOUGH, GENETIC MAKEUP AND DNA CODING WILL NOT CHANGE.

Genetic predisposition does not mean that it is guaranteed that the offspring will be affected by the diseases or traits of the parental genes, but, it may likely develop in some varying degree.

Genetic changes and variations contribute to the causes of genetic diseases but the likelihood of these diseases is not absolutely certain. It has been known that in the same family with several siblings, the predisposed genetic variation will affect some siblings but may not affect others.

An improved lifestyle, healthy food eating habits, regular exercises, maintaining a healthy weight and body mass index (BMI) will certainly be beneficial. Staying away from smoking (even passive smoking) drug and alcohol abuse will provide improvement to DNA's healthy surroundings. Environmental conditions such as excessive radiation from sun and sunburns and too many lifestyle stresses should be avoided at all costs. All these good practices to keep a healthy body and mind will go a long way to improve the overall health and well-being.

Anatomically, ageing process involves several changes in our organs and the systems within our body.

Let us look at age-related changes in a more detailed but generalised way for easy understanding.

The first visible sign under the normal ageing process is the change in our appearance, our hair is greying and we may start shedding hair strands in clumps, we often lose our upright posture from our youthful years, our tooth decay may also show up and our skin anatomy undergoes marked changes.

Folks, do not despair as this is the law of Nature and eventually, we become one with Nature.

Skin is our largest external organ which practically covers the whole of our body. Our skin has several layers, the outermost layer the Epidermis begins to thin out due to the deterioration in the cellular integrity. The outermost skin layer sheds around 2g of dead cells every day. In young adults, the lost skin cells are replenished at a much faster rate than in an elderly person which exacerbates thinning in the skin structure.

The appearance of sagging skin and wrinkles are also very common signs of ageing skin which are usually caused by the dryness of the skin, lack of proteins (especially elastin), nutrients e.g., collagen and fatty acids from the dermis and the subcutaneous layers both of which are sub-epidermis layers of our skin. Age-related dryness of the skin is often due to the decline in the activities of the sweat glands and oil glands both located in the epidermis and the dermis layer. This results in the outermost layer of our skin, the epidermis not getting enough moisture and lubrication giving it a dry and rough appearance. Lack of moisture also causes loss in the body's temperature control. The sweat glands provide the outer layer of our skin with sweat (moisture) which then evaporates causing a cooling effect. So, we can say it is like an internal Air-conditioning system that with aging becomes inefficient. The further implication of this is, that our skin can be damaged easily, with minor cracks and bruising likely to appear, that can take much longer to mend.

There are several non-anatomical reasons for skin damage in the elderly such as the effects of medication (e.g., topical application of steroids), the effect of excess UV radiation, environmental pollution, and often overlooked effects of the harsh and corrosive chemicals from the cosmetic application on the skin.

Our skin, young or aged, is very sensitive and can damage easily but it is quite resilient too and heals quickly thanks to the process of rejuvenation of the dead cells are faster in younger than in older skin.

Lack of natural pigmentation and natural protective effects of the ageing skin can cause irreversible damage. This has a detrimental effect on temperature regulation, vitamin D synthesis, impaired new cell growth, storage and synthesis of essential bio-chemicals e.g., fatty acids, proteins, collagen and essentially the integrity of blood vessels and capillaries which are located under the bottom layer of the dermis. This will eventually lead to higher stress levels on the aged skin causing visible age or liver spots, itch and eczema, and fragile blood vessels causing them to bruise easily and haemorrhage.

During my research on various aspects of inclusions in this book I found the topic of "Genetic Disorder" in Wikipedia with a lot of useful information; very well presented. I present here some interesting facts from that reference for all to read; the diagram is well presented and thought out by the original author; unfortunately, I was unable to view the original article to acknowledge the original author. (Gratefully referenced. *https://en.wikipedia.org/wiki/Genetic_disorder*)

It has been reported (*OMIM Gene Map Statistics". www.omim.org. Retrieved 2020-01-14*) that there are in excess of 6000 known genetic disorders and new disorders are continually being discovered. It is also reported (*March 2021 "An online compendium of treatable genetic disorders". American Journal of Medical Genetics. Part C, Seminars in Medical Genetics.* ***187*** *(1): 48–54*) that more than 600 genetic disorders are treatable, good news indeed but more needs to be done to increase the treatable numbers.

The following diagram features examples of a disease located on each chromosome.

(https://en.wikipedia.org/wiki/Genetic_disorder)

Noteworthy and of interest are;

- Alzheimer's disease located at chromosome 14
- Cystic fibrosis at 7
- Breast cancer at 17
- Muscular dystrophy at 19
- Polycystic kidney disease at 16

- Phenyl-ketone urea at 12
- Melanoma at 9 and so on; interesting

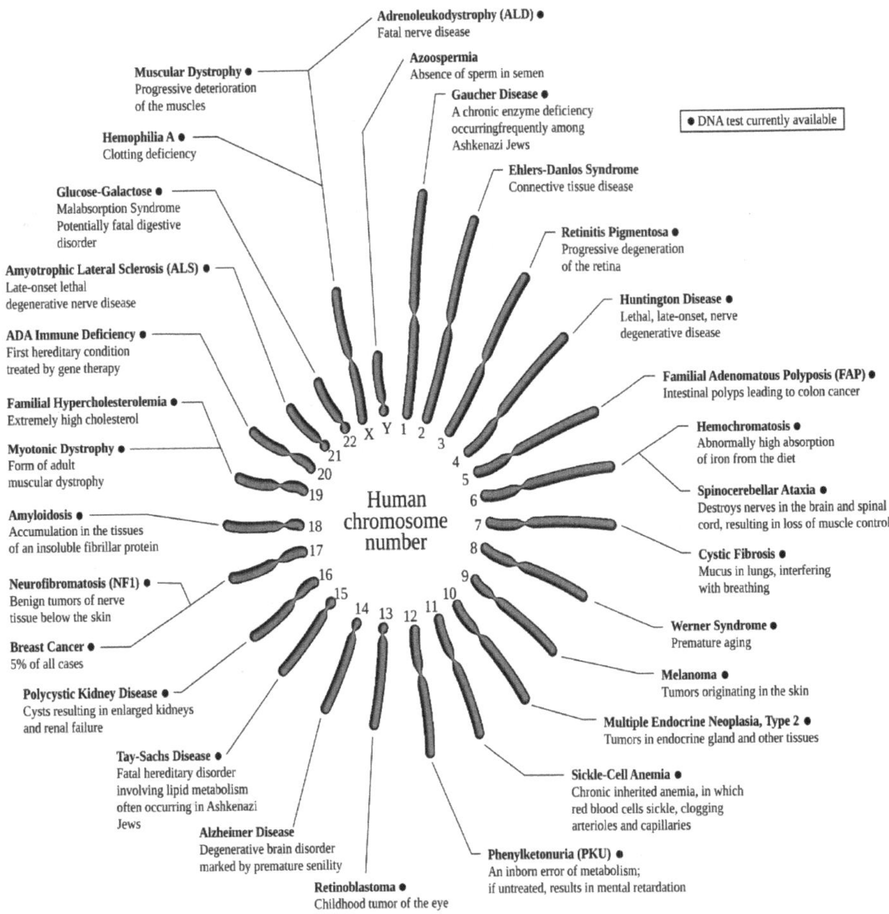

As we know now gene mutations primarily cause genetic disorders, it can be either mutation in a single gene or multiple genes. This gene mutation can also be due to the environment such as the effect of radiation, chemical pollution e.g. pesticides, carcinogenic breakdown of foods and drug intakes and several other factors.

There is also a greater risk of gene mutations from bacterial and viral infections.

Chromosomal abnormality is also a significant reason for genetic disorders e.g. defective chromosomes 7 and 21 produce Williams Syndrome and Down syndrome.

Statistically, it has been reported (*2001, Mayo Clinic Proceedings.* ***76*** *(8): 777–783*) that 1 in 50 people is affected by a known single-gene disorder and around 1 in 263 are affected by a chromosomal disorder.

Fountain of Youth

Oh yes! The fountain of youth; over many centuries people have been searching for that mythical spring which is alleged to have healing powers for those who drink it or bathe in it. Early crusaders in the 11th and 12th centuries and stories of Prester John a legendary king gave some credence to stories of the mythical spring among the people of that time.

In the early 16th century, The Caribbean island people also believed in this mythical story and spoke of the magical powers of the waters from a mythical place called Bimini. Actually, Bimini islands do exist and is the further most Westerly place in the Bahamas about 80 Kilometres East of Miami. The story became more powerful when the Spanish explorer, and the first governor of Puerto Rico, Juan Ponce de León was told of the existence of such a mystical place in Bimini by the Native Americans. Whether Juan Ponce de León found the fountain of youth is another story.

But the legend does not end here. The Greek historian Herodotus, also known as the "Father of History" who lived around the 5th century BC wrote about an African tribe who were known for their long lives and youthful appearance. He wrote about this pool of mythical water with magical powers.

Alexander the Great (b. 356 BC – d. 323 BC) being very curious and inquisitive about the so-called fountain of youth, searched for it.

But has anyone found it?

There may have been a stream or a river tributary in ancient time with clean pure water running down a mountain pass which had a clean pure taste which ancient people dubbed as the fountain of youth. These days there is commercial mileage to be gained out of this mythical story unfortunately with no scientific validation or credibility. An archaeological park in St. Augustine one of the oldest cities in the state of Florida in U.S.A. has been created to commemorate the arrival of Juan Ponce de León in 1513.

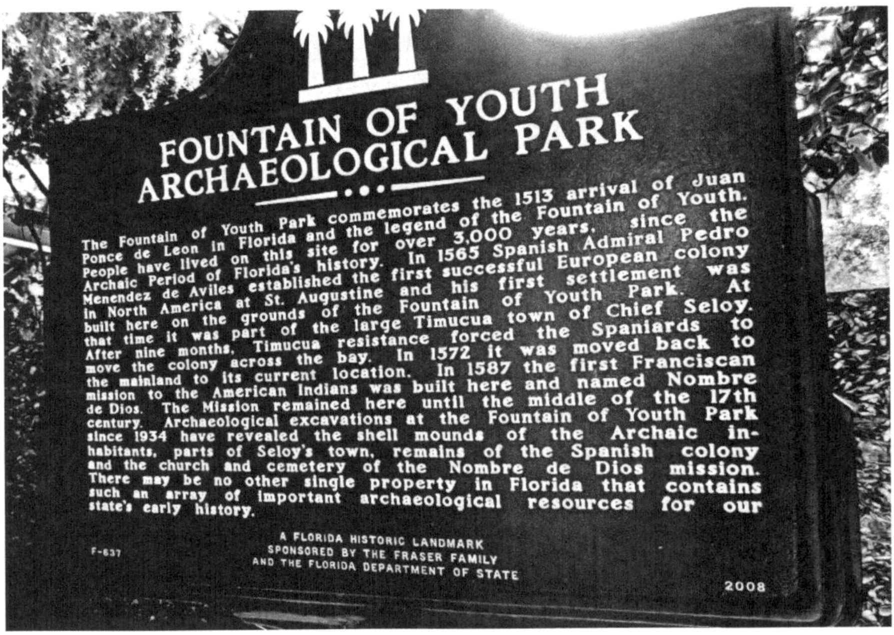

Photo by: Christa Thompson
(https://www.nationalgeographic.com/history/article/fountain-of-youth)

My last thoughts on the Fountain of Youth!

No, I have not found it. I have stopped looking for it. But I can theorize as to what it could be.

As we look at the various stages of our lifecycle we can look at ageing in a different perspective.

Let us assume that we have achieved what we set out to achieve by the age of 60 years, when we are still reasonably *"healthy wealthy and wise"*. Give or take a few years as we all are biologically unique and have different outlooks on life; glass half full or half empty kind of perception.

The fountain of youth is within us and all we have to do is to explore it and look at our life in a positive frame of mind. It takes a lot of positivity to overcome negativity in our life amidst doom and gloom that we often hear of but what can be done? Except, seek the fountain of youth in all of us.

In the words of the beautiful actress of the 1960's "There is a fountain of youth: it is your mind, your talents, the creativity you bring to your life and the lives of the people you love. When you learn to tap this source, you will truly have defeated age." ~ Sophia Loren

Chapter 3

AGE RELATED COGNITIVE AND MENTAL IMPAIRMENT

"We all live in hope—young and old alike—but we the seniors, who have fulfilled that hope, are well ahead in life's race."

– Jay Das … 2024

As I think about ageing and contemplate on my old age, I do appreciate life and what has been given to me. I have crossed the age barrier of 75 years and running into my 76th; I can only count my blessings. I have a lovely caring family and an independent lifestyle and the future ahead looks good unless something or some unforeseen events come crashing down on me. But the future is in the future and thinking of the negatives can only cause misery and despair.

What is contemplation

Contemplation is awakening our mind. It brings us closer to our inner thoughts, feeling of joy, being one with nature, and broadening our minds to accept different views and rational thoughts. There is nothing tangible about contemplation, it does not have any physical existence. It is all in our mind and contemplation just stimulates the inner core. However, contemplation is not only positive thoughts but also fear, trials and tribulations, challenges in life and a test of our patience and courage. To a weaker mind it can bring out the worst: a conflict between good and evil.

To senior citizens like us, contemplation is a good life skill to have. All that is needed is some free and peaceful time to reflect upon your past and present and think of the future. A lot of benefit can be had by practicing contemplation at our age. It improves our power of concentration and mental focus which is lacking as we age. Seniors can be helped by practicing contemplation in many ways. Improves self-esteem: This is sadly lacking as we age. As we lose our various faculties, our hearing, vision, power of speech, presence of mind and few other positive life skills we become lonely and withdrawn and our self-confidence suffers. Self-esteem breeds into us confidence and power of self-realization as to who we are and what our goal is. Contemplation also improves self-awareness and builds up our conscious mind to be aware and alert of the situations and circumstances around us. It also raises our inner strength, and improves our skills to deal with various situations which we otherwise would have found difficult to deal with. It improves self-discipline and problem-solving abilities which are valuable assets in our old age and most urgently needed. All these and more positive attributes can help in stress reduction and minor physiological and psychological difficulties which are of non-medical nature and do not require medical interventions. But please remember that any physical and mental discomforts experienced at any time must be medically attended to, rather than wait for our psyche to heal by itself or by contemplative practices. I, therefore, consider contemplation and reflection as a very powerful, non-invasive tools to build up our inner-strength to face challenges that old age presents to us; we look upon our failures and mistakes in proper context ….. Having no regrets. This is also a way to successfully Ageing Gracefully.

Contemplation brings out the best in us in our golden years, look at it with happiness, joy, positive expectations and freedom to charter your own path and goals. Have a meaningful life being active and being aware of your surroundings.

According to the World Health Organization (WHO), mental health is "a state of well-being in which the individual can realize his or her abilities, can cope with the normal stresses of life, can work productively and fruitfully, and can contribute to his or her community" (*Ref: World Health Organization promoting mental health: concepts, emerging evidence, practice (Summary Report) Geneva: World Health Organization; 2004.*).

Cognitive and mental health:

This is perhaps one of the serious and delicate disability that many seniors go through as they progress into their senior years. This is also the time when lack of suitable care and loneliness can push them to the very edge of death or despair. Cognitive impairment and Mental Health can be grouped under one umbrella and treated under a wide range of issues such as Alzheimer's disease, dementia, bipolar disorder and many more. Approximately 15% of the global adult population aged 60 and over suffer from a mental disorder of some kind; this almost amounts to around 140-150 million people according to population statistics WHO (2017). In the United States alone over 5 million people above the age of 65 suffer from depression. In Australia this number is between 10 and 15 per cent of older people experience depression (around 400,000 seniors).

There are several warning trigger points that can initiate mental anxiety and depression among elderly citizens:

Loneliness and disruption to the regular care routine can be the precursors to mental health issues.

The feeling of Loneliness can affect young adults and older adults alike. The very thought of abandonment and lack of friendships can affect young adults in their future years and become a permanent drawback in their advancement unless a meaningful intervention by family, friends and especially their peer group is initiated. Withdrawal symptoms can lead young adults astray and commit them to undesirable activities, often to the point of no return.

Older people are also at a high risk of facing loneliness and social isolation. This may be due to several reasons for example living alone without strong social connections or ties, lack of social and communal activities, living in isolation in institutions due to prolonged illnesses, living in retirement homes but due to their ethnicity, race or other backgrounds remain isolated due to a severe lack of communication skills, etc. Some older adults due to no family or recent death of friends and partners can go into self-isolation from where a return to normality can be time-consuming regardless of quality care intervention. It is important that under these special and delicate situations quality care intervention must take place at the earliest signs of withdrawal symptoms. Unattended cases of loneliness can lead to mental illness and suffering in the long run. Older people are also very accustomed to their set environment and sometimes are very difficult to accommodate any meaningful change, and why not? As seniors we have contributed a lot to our community and society and have earned the right to live out our life as graciously and comfortably as possible. Institutionalised elders are often very attached to their care group and any change to the care regime and caregiver can have a detrimental effect on their health and well-being.

It is hard to distinguish cognitive impairments from mental health from an academic point of view as both may be accommodated under the scope of Brain health. However, the most simplified definition of cognitive impairment would be the lack of our ability to learn, think, analyse and retain bits and pieces of information, both new and old and process them to be used appropriately. This would broadly entail learning disabilities, mental capacity, and to certain extent memory functions. On the other hand, mental health delves deeper into the brain function and invokes our emotional and psychological status.

Mental health is not age-related but, can be of significance and importance at every stage of our life from our childhood right through to senior years and must never be ignored.

Cognitive impairment (CI) is not a disease or sickness. In young people, lack of attention and learning difficulties may contribute significantly to CI and can be helped with a good diet, vitamin therapy and also, care and management.

In older people CI can be of a more serious nature and may not be reversible due to declining brain function, inadequate nutrition, certain infections (e.g., urinary tract infection), respiratory complications (e.g., Pneumonia), dehydration, adverse effect to certain medication (particularly overuse of anti-depressants, opiate medications, etc.), stroke resulting in paralysis, speech impairment, dementia, etc.

When we age our brain functions decrease resulting in many cognitive issues. We lose the power and the aptitude to process data with ease and speed as we have done in our younger days. This happens primarily due to the measurable alteration in the brain structure and chemistry which maintains the functionality and data processing power of human activity. Our brain is a complex structure and let us compare it to a computer. When a computer's data processor becomes slow due to age it can be easily replaced with a fresh data card or a memory chip. But, an ageing human brain cannot be updated like a computer and we have to live with the loss of neuron structure (nerve cells) which sends and receives signals from various parts of our body to carry out movement activities and also the data processing activities. These neurons vary in their data handling and messaging (receiving and sending) assignments, for example, some process sensory activities and therefore sections of these neurons (also called **sensory neurons**) are assigned for hearing, vision, touch, smell, etc.

There is a second kind of neurons called the **motor neurons** which are assigned to other every day functional abilities which send and receive signals to and from our organs, muscular system and also our glands.

All information and the processing of the signals received from and sent to various parts of our body are processed in the Central Nervous System (CNS) situated in the brain attached to the spinal cord where the interneurons are active.

With aging the size of our brain also decreases (*Harada et. al, Normal cognitive aging. Clin Geriatr Med. 2013; 29(4):737–752*), resulting in a decline in the neuron functions which causes the slowing down of signalling leading to specific organ, gland, muscle and sensory impairment.

Cognitive impairment and Cognitive decline have the same meaning and are pertinent to explaining a sudden or gradual change in the data-processing function of the brain in the elderly.

Depending on the underlying cause, this may become a temporary lapse in attention or concentration, a more permanent decline.

Recent researches have suggested that a healthy and active lifestyle can markedly slow down the ageing process and delay the onset of cognitive impairment.

One of the main reasons for cognitive impairment in the elderly is the weakening of brain function and neural activities. This comes with the fact that our body and mind both get lazy for whatever reason and go into a state of inertia.

With all due respect, I am not denigrating an elderly person's brain activity, it is a fact of life, and we have to think of ways to reinvigorate the lethargic or sluggish brain.

Quoting from my previous book, "Let Your Organs Breathe," let me put forward a few important activities which could help improve the mental activity level.

- Although there may not be a cure to enhance our cognitive health after a certain age, but it has been widely reported that by making some lifestyle adjustments improvements can be noticeable.
- There are a number of activities that may be considered to enhance our cognitive skills; some of these can practiced in our old age.
- Mental Stimulation:

- Challenge yourself with memory games and stay alert. Solving puzzles, simple mathematical equations, and mental games that require thinking such as remembering people and places you may have visited in the distant past, birth dates etc. There can be any number of life memories that can be brought to life by the power of remembrance.
- Reading, learning and creating new things.
- Allowing your brain to have adequate rest with peaceful sleep.
- Engage in Stimulating conversations and discussions on current topics of interest.
- Exercises which will stimulate flow of blood in your body and also your brain, such as mild running, tread milling, etc.
- Dietary adjustments:
- To improve blood sugar, cholesterol and triglyceride levels and control blood pressure
- Avoiding abuse or misuse of alcohol, drugs and tobacco.
- Mental Health:
- Try to build up social network, keeping in-touch with friends and relatives to ease loneliness and try to minimise emotional stresses.
- Undertake group walks or walk with a companion, a friend or a pet.
- Light physical exercises such as swimming, free hand exercises as mentioned in Chapter 5 will help to pass the time, listen to music, read books, etc. All these will certainly help and lead towards the path of fulfilment and enjoyment.
- Playing cards and board games with family and friends can have a great positive outcome.
- Device your own challenges and move forward; it could be inch by inch or could be in leaps and bounds. Every bit helps.
- Adequate hydration

Mental health

It is a medical condition just like other common conditions; Diabetes, cardiovascular disease, blood pressure, etc., and can be treated both by using drugs and psychiatric interventions. The treatment of mental health is a highly specialized and individualized regimen and requires a treatment plan which takes into consideration the severity of the symptoms and the general health and well-being of the patient. It is also a highly sensitive area and must require the patient's consent before any external involvements are included in the treatment plan. Good nutrition, vitamin therapy, adequate rest and relaxation for the individual and a positive lifestyle change, including exercise, are important for the recovery process.

A general understanding of mental health issues, symptoms and the quality of care provided by the primary carers and the support team is of prime consideration in the management of mental health.

Some facts on mental health and seniors as published by Pan American Health Organization (PAHO) and the World Health Organization (WHO) (Ref: *https://www3.paho.org/hq/index.php?option=com_contentandview=articleandid=9877:seniors-mental-healthandItemid=0andlang=en*), may be of some help in coping with this condition in some elderly people. It is also noted that Depression is the most common mental health problem in older people and more than 65% of the older population do not get the proper treatment that they require. It is also reported that mental health issues are a common occurrence among older people who are lonely and isolated and as such many suffer from a state of confusion, disorientation and an enhanced state of dementia, psychosis, etc., which contributes in addition to their physical state of health and well-being. Medical intervention is absolutely necessary under these circumstances, as it has been reported that People aged 85 and older have the highest suicide and self-harm rate of any age group. The management of Mental

Health conditions is a highly specialized area with frequent Psychiatric and medical interventions necessary.

Stimulating brain function is also a positive activity and may help in the recovery. Those who are interested in computer games can do so by downloading a few fun games, which I found interesting.

(*Ref:https://assistinghands.com/20/illinois/hinsdale/blog/best-online-games-for-seniors/*).

I am simply assuming that in this highly developed digital age that we live in, many of us are equipped with very basic computer literacy to handle simple computer games that have been specially devised for us seniors. Besides computer games, there are many other manual "brain teasers" which could be downloaded and worked on to stimulate brain functions.

Renewing social ties and bonding with fellow seniors is important along with partaking in happy and joyous social activities; at the same time, keeping up with good nutrition is a step in the right direction.

There have been many food items suggested to help brain activity and function. Just to summarise, a few items listed below may be of benefit. It is also generally recognised that components like omega-3 fatty acids, B vitamins, and antioxidants are known to support brain health and are often referred to as brain foods. Research shows that the best brain foods are the same ones that protect your heart and blood vessels, including the following: **Green leafy vegetables:** Kale, spinach, broccoli, carrots, etc., are rich in brain-healthy nutrients like vitamin K, lutein, folic acid, and beta carotene and the mixed carotenoids. **Fatty fish:** Fatty fish which are good sources of omega-3 fatty acids, such as Salmon, Mackerel, Gem fish, Tuna, etc., are a healthy source of good fats (unsaturated fats). There is endless supply of these and other fish like Sardines in Australia and they have been linked to lowering the levels of beta-amyloid Peptides in the brains of people with Alzheimer's disease. **Berries:** Berries contain flavonoids and anthocyanin, the blue to purple pigments of blueberries, blackberries, etc. These are good antioxidants and improve circulation; researchers at Brigham and Women's Hospital found that women who consumed two or more servings of strawberries and blueberries each week delayed memory decline by up to two-and-a-half years (*published in Annals of Neurology 2012*). Brigham and Women's Hospital in Boston is a major teaching hospital of Harvard Medical School. **Tea and coffee:** In a study *published in The Journal of Nutrition (2014) researchers at Johns Hopkins University* reported that taking 200mg caffeine tablets had a better effect on mental function. It may therefore seem that a cup of morning tea or Coffee could offer not just a short term boost but also some long term memory enhancement. **Walnuts:** Nuts are healthy food and may help with memory improvements. A 2015 study from UCLA linked higher walnut consumption to improved cognitive test scores. The reason given was walnuts are a rich source of alpha-linolenic acid (ALA) which helps blood pressure and protects arteries, parameters good for the heart and brain. (*Ref: Food linked to better brain power Harvard Health www.health.harvard.edu*).

Further reading references:

- A Guide to Cognitive Fitness, a Special Health Report from Harvard Medical School.
- 11 Best Foods to Boost Your Brain and Memory - Health line ttps:// www.healthline.com " nutrition).

Different seniors age at a different rate. Some seem to age very rapidly, while others experience aging at a much more gradual pace. Often, we meet someone who appears to be much younger or older as the case may be than their appearance and their chronological age. The cause for this could be hereditary or self-awareness and good management. Also, our ageing process may largely depend on the internal functioning of our organs and the way we think. We briefly touched upon our sensory decline as we age (chapter 2). These changes are a normal part of ageing with the ageing process of our organs. For example, the weakening of our eyesight can be due to thickening of the lenses in our eyes. The clear fluid called the vitreous which fills the space between the lens of our eyes and the retina starts to dry up with age causing separation of the light-sensitive fibres in the vitreous and retina causing vision impairment to a certain degree. Similarly, Hearing loss is a common old-age condition that we tend to suffer on a gradual basis as we age.

There can be several reasons for this such as damage to the anatomy of the inner year, ear infections, ear drum perforation and more often a gradual build-up of wax. All these can affect hearing loss and can be rectified in varying degrees unless the damage to the ear's anatomy is more permanent.

Ageing process and dependencies:

Ageing process has several variables. The below diagram reflects the eight quadrants of dependencies. Any one, or, several dependencies may contribute to the acceleration of the ageing process. Delaying the dependency would delay the ageing process and help seniors lead a satisfactory life. These dependencies if addressed adequately can trigger awareness in seniors of the negative effects of these dependencies and promote self-management and instincts. Let us now see how the above eight quadrants contribute to the ageing process and lifestyle. However, it needs to be mentioned that many elderly people in our community live alone and have adjusted their lifestyle according to their immediate status.

Ageing Process and Eight Quadrants of Dependency:

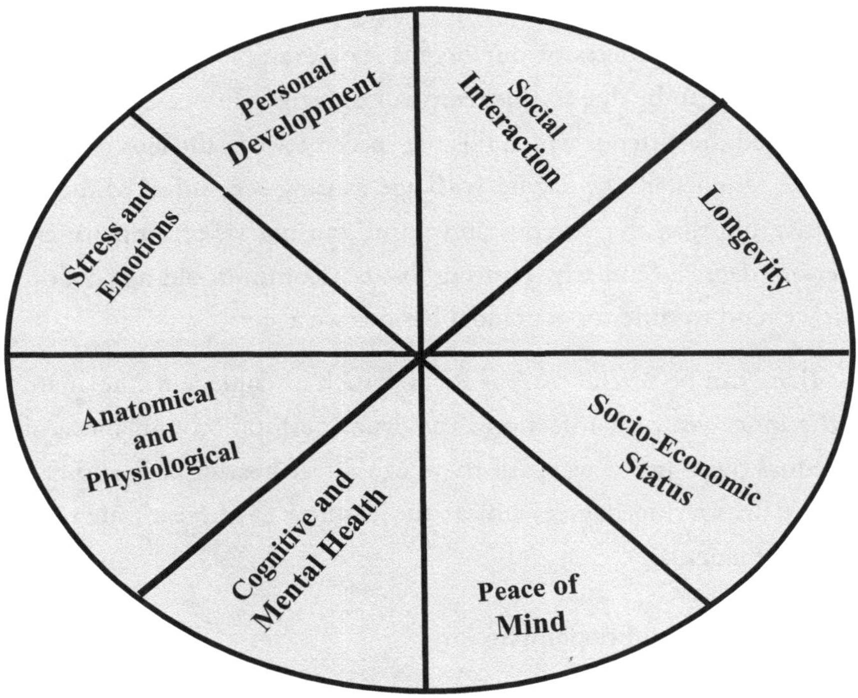

- **Social interaction:** Lack of social interaction can be very distressing and affects a senior citizen's lifestyle in a much negative way. It also contributes to loneliness and has a strong psychological effect from where recovery may be difficult or too slow without professional intervention. This dependency can manifest in the form of mild mental dis-balance and should not be considered as a normal symptom of ageing process.

Several reported study results have shown that elderly citizens who lack social interaction tend to have more health problems than those who are not socially isolated.

- **Stress and emotions:** Mental and Emotional stress can be a very powerful detriment to our general health and well-being. It can affect the population at any age group. Young adults can bounce back from this state because of their diverse activity and peer support but in senior adults it can leave a lasting negative impression from which recovery may be quite slow and generally requires professional and caring intervention. Studies have shown that there can be several warning signs in adults such as general feeling of tiredness, insomnia and restlessness, frequent head, shoulder and muscle aches and pains, lack of concentration and others. Some or many of these general symptoms may be manifestation of other health issues and should not be ignored or taken lightly.

- **Personal development:** There may be a subtle noticeable change in behavioural patterns. Seniors appear to be withdrawn and often apologetic for simple or no reasons at all. Some of this may be attributable to dementia memory loss and loss of brain functions.

Our brain plays a pivotal role in our personal development and personality changes. Various lobes or simply areas of the brain have different functions.

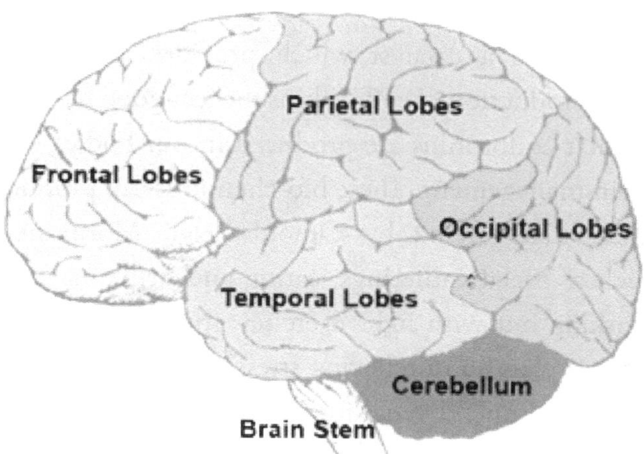

(Ref: www.health.qld.gov.au/abios/asp/boccipital; Acquired Brain Injury Outreach Service (ABIOS)

Frontal lobe, as the name suggests, sits at the front of the brain and controls the personality traits, decision making and movements. It is also associated with our speech ability.

Parietal lobe is situated in the middle part of the brain structure and is primarily concerned with the sensory aspects including perception, integration and the management of our various senses e.g. taste, hearing, sight, touch, and smell. It is also responsible for our sense of temperature, pressure and pain.

Occipital lobe sits at the back of the head and is responsible for visual perception, including colour, form and motion.

Temporal lobe is located under the Parietal lobe and at the back of the ears. It is responsible for the processing of auditory information, short term memory, language and emotional feelings. It also facilitates rhythms and musical interpretations.

- **Peace of mind:** Peace of mind is an important aspect of our general health and well-being at any age let alone only in the elderly people's health condition.

Mental peace is a catalyst which provides a sense of calmness promoting the production of endorphins the feel-good hormones. Studies have shown that endorphins are produced in our bodies in response to stress and pain management. These bio-chemicals can produce a stronger response than that offered by Opioids, e.g., Morphine. Feel-good activities such as social gatherings, eating and drinking in moderation, cooking, working out with light exercises, intimacy with your partner, etc., can act as a placebo in relieving stress, anxiety, and restlessness and bring peace and calmness. Laughing also has a wonderful placebo effect and helps trigger the release of endorphins (*Ref: J Neurosci. 2017 Jun 21; 37(25):6125-6131 and J Exp Med. 2016 Jul; 239(3):243-9*). As the saying goes "Laughter is the best medicine"; a short laughter session with family and friends can often work wonders to create the peace and calmness in mind to help temporarily mend several simple mental issues.

- **Socio-economic Status:** According to World Health Organization (WHO) by 2030 the population of elderly people will jump to about 16.7% and by 2050 this figure is likely to rise to almost 22%. 80% of these elderly citizens are likely to be living in some form of socio-economic dilemma. Many of the older population living in countries with low per capita income do find themselves below the poverty line and find it hard to survive with not much societal or government assistance.

At a general Assembly resolution (46/91), 16 December 1991 United Nations Principles for Older Persons in recognition of their services to their communities a charter was prepared detailing certain basic human rights principles (*Ref: www.org/en/instruments-mechanisms/instruments/United-nations-principles-older-persons*).

The Charter as agreed upon, passed and documented is referred to below; it certainly makes a good read, but I wonder how much or how many of the 18 points have been adhered to or put into practice.

1. Older persons should have access to adequate food, water, shelter, clothing and health care through the provision of income, family and community support and self-help.
2. Older persons should have the opportunity to work or to have access to other income-generating opportunities.
3. Older persons should be able to participate in determining when and at what pace withdrawal from the labour force takes place.
4. Older persons should have access to appropriate educational and training programmes.
5. Older persons should be able to live in environments that are safe and adaptable to personal preferences and changing capacities.

6. Older persons should be able to reside at home for as long as possible.
7. Older persons should remain integrated in society, participate actively in the formulation and implementation of policies that directly affect their well-being and share their knowledge and skills with younger generations.
8. Older persons should be able to seek and develop opportunities for service to the community and to serve as volunteers in positions appropriate to their interests and capabilities.
9. Older persons should be able to form movements or associations of older persons.
10. Older persons should benefit from family and community care and protection in accordance with each society's system of cultural values.
11. Older persons should have access to health care to help them to maintain or regain the optimum level of physical, mental and emotional well-being and to prevent or delay the onset of illness.
12. Older persons should have access to social and legal services to enhance their autonomy, protection and care.
13. Older persons should be able to utilize appropriate levels of institutional care providing protection, rehabilitation and social and mental stimulation in a humane and secure environment.
14. Older persons should be able to enjoy human rights and fundamental freedoms when residing in any shelter, care or treatment facility, including full respect for their dignity, beliefs, needs and privacy and for the right to make decisions about their care and the quality of their lives.
15. Older persons should be able to pursue opportunities for the full development of their potential.
16. Older persons should have access to the educational, cultural, spiritual and recreational resources of society.

17. Older persons should be able to live in dignity and security and be free of exploitation and physical or mental abuse.
18. Older persons should be treated fairly regardless of age, gender, racial or ethnic background, disability or other status, and be valued independently of their economic contribution.

This charter is quite comprehensive and well prepared, but the saddest part is what now, who is going to enforce it and who is going to champion the cause of the elderly people in accordance to the United Nations Charter.

In many poorer and under-developed countries with high pressure and stress of day-to-day living many older people think it is a curse to live beyond a certain age when their physical and mental faculties are still active and they can live with some dignity. It is a hopeless and sad situation.

In developed nations there are organizations which do keep a watch on older citizens in conjunction with government welfare departments for their wellbeing. At least this vigilance helps maintain some sort of positivity among the older people in the sunset period of their live.

- **Cognitive and mental health:** This is perhaps one of the serious and delicate disability that many seniors go through as they progress into their senior years. This is also the time when lack of suitable care and loneliness can push them to the very edge of death or despair. Cognitive impairment and Mental Health can be grouped under one umbrella and treated under a wide range of issues such as Alzheimer's disease, dementia, bipolar disorder and many more. Approximately 15% of the global adult population aged 60 and over suffer from a mental disorder; this almost amounts to around 140-150 million people according to population statistics WHO (2017). In the United States alone over 5 million people above the age of 65 suffer from depression.

In Australia this number is between 10 and 15 per cent of older people experience depression (around 400,000 seniors).

There are several warning trigger points that can initiate mental anxiety and depression among elderly citizens:

Loneliness, and disruption to the regular care routine can be the precursors to mental health issues.

The feeling of **Loneliness** can affect young adults and older adults alike. The very thought of abandonment and lack of friendships can affect young adults in their future years and become a permanent drawback in their advancement unless a meaningful intervention by family, friends and especially their peer group is initiated. Withdrawal symptoms can lead young adults astray and commit them to undesirable activities often to the point of no return.

Older people are also at a high risk of facing loneliness and social isolation. This may be due to several reasons for example living alone without strong social connections or ties, lack of social and communal activities, living in isolation in institutions due to prolonged illnesses, living in retirement homes but due to their ethnic, racial or other backgrounds remain isolated due to a severe lack of communication skills etc. Some older adults due to no family or recent death of friends and partners can go into self-isolation from where a return to normality can be time-consuming regardless of care intervention. It is important that under these special and delicate situations quality care intervention must take place at the earliest signs of withdrawal symptoms. Unattended cases of loneliness can lead to mental illness and suffering in the long run. Older people are also very accustomed to their set environment and sometimes are very difficult to change, and why not? As seniors we have contributed a lot to our community and society and have earned the right to live out our life as graciously and comfortably as possible. Institutionalised elders are often very attached to their care group and any change to the care regime and caregiver can have a detrimental effect in their health and well-being.

- **Anatomical and physiological status:** Ageing process is invariably associated with declining health characterized by degeneration in body's organ system. Deterioration in the health of one or several organs resulting in systemic failures may affect the Physiological functionality.

Some individuals with a stronger constitution may be able to cope with the deteriorating organ or organ system with age and thus are more prepared to face physiological challenges and functional decline. The ageing process initiates a biological change which impacts the cellular structure at a cellular level causing damage to our organs and tissues at a varying degree. This, over a period of time impacts our various physiological faculties and diminishes their functionality. Although this gradual decline in physiological functionality is not reversible but may be slowed down with adequate nutrition, exercise and mental conditioning.

Some of the anatomical and physiological concerns have been addressed briefly earlier in the chapter. In the next couple of chapters we will look at in a bit more details anatomical and physiological effects and ageing.

- **Longevity:** Everybody wants to live a long and fruitful life. Longevity perhaps sums up all dependencies in our ageing process. Longevity gives a focus and a purpose in live and therefore we all tend to consciously or sub-consciously do things which would help us live longer for example some of us in our senior years become more attached to our grandchildren, undertake some form of social work, involve in communal activities and part-take in many more activities which are little bit removed from their regular social interactions for example they themselves become quasi care-givers to their elderly peer group who are in a more delicate stage of their life. Life expectancy gains or increase in longevity among a group of seniors could have both positive and challenging societal issues. For example, it may prove to be a complex set of circumstances when applying for general insurance and more particularly in securing travel insurances which may be denied or offered at a much higher rate of age-related premium.

The society needs to undertake to facilitate the transition of seniors in their 70s to 80s and beyond in such a way that progressive seniors in their 80s and more are not inconvenienced. Research in social studies points out to the fact that in most countries not only limited to underdeveloped countries but also affluent countries around the globe almost 30% of the senior population is lonely and deprived of social connectivity. This can have serious physical and mental implications and could affect their longevity.

Most of the dependencies are manageable with self-awareness, good nutrition and proper professional care and medical intervention. Although ageing process is not reversible, but with care and consideration towards our ageing population a lot can be achieved to make progress into the ageing lifecycle more pleasant and meaningful for seniors to live with dignity and comfort.

Signs of cognitive decline in old age: It is a general anatomical phenomenon that as we age most of our organs tend to shrink. Our brain structure undergoes this shrinkage too and there is a consistent decline in the information retrieval part of the brain. There are many other subtle changes in our brain function which result in forgetfulness lack of cohesiveness etc. Some of the early signs of cognitive decline are as follows. The most important change is that the sufferer may not realise these changes, but they are quite noticeable to others, especially family and friends. Difficulty remembering places or events caused by temporary or even short term memory lapses are also concerning signs. Directional confusion; is also quite common. Cognitively impaired sufferers in many instances lose the directional concept and tend to forget where they are heading to even though they may have visited the same destination several times. There is a little structure deep inside the brain called hippocampus which is responsible for memory, learning and navigational skills. The hippocampus can be affected by neurological and psychiatric disorders. Temporary lack or short-term memory loss: Signs are; forgetfulness in remembering names and places visited Missing dates, appointments and social events, difficulty in continuation or keeping up with a conversation etc. Additionally, exercising poor judgement due to short-term memory loss, loss of sense of direction while driving or getting around places and many other minor discrepancies from normal day-to-day activities where memory plays a key part. A more serious form of mild cognitive impairment (MCI) is when your friends and family notice changes in your behavioural pattern, e.g., increase in aggressiveness, mild depression and anxiety and in general a lack of participation and interest. Any of the above signs and several more are indications of cognitive impairment and medical intervention to provide a care regime for the wellbeing of the patients must be put in place.

Following activities and lifestyle improvements can help.

- Regular exercise and keeping busy
- A diet rich in omega-3 fatty acids, fruits and green leafy vegetables
- Reading books playing card and board games
- Playing musical instruments, developing a hobby
- Maintaining a regular sleep pattern
- Attending memory training workshops.

Causes of cognitive decline The reasons are multi-dimensional and vary from mild to severe impairment. The following reasons are important to watch out for and patient condition reviewed periodically so that a management plan can be executed while keeping the patient's well-being in mind.

1. Side effects from prescribed medications:

This is a very important consideration as several prescribed drugs can have a temporary or even a long-term effect on a patient's mental and cognitive state. For example, Dementia Australia in a recent publication (*https://www.dementia.org.au/sites/default/files/helpsheets/Helpsheet-DementiaQandA25_Benzodiazepines_englis*) has suggested that Benzodiazepines should be used with caution, particularly in patients who have cognitive impairment or who are over the age of 60 years. It has also been published (*Exploratory Research in Clinical and Social Pharmacy Volume 3, September 2021, 100054*) that Benzodiazepine can have increased risk of sedation, cognitive impairment, delirium and fall in older people.

2. Deficiencies of important nutrients:

Malnutrition is a common underlying cause of nutrient deficiency in older people. There are many references in reputable journals highlighting this fact, e.g., in a 2016 publication (*Ageing Res Rev. 2016 Nov; 31: 80–92.*) it has been reported that glucose deficiency due to lack of quality carbohydrates in the diet may reduce the available energy needed for the brain to improve the cognitive processes and performances.

3. Alcohol, drug use, and cognitive health in the elderly

Older adults experience age-related physiological changes that significantly diminishes their ability to metabolize alcohol, recreational drugs, and many prescription medications. Also, smoking can be very detrimental to their health and wellbeing. The decline in their metabolic efficiency causes an elevation of toxins within their body which increases the risk of toxicity and adverse reactions far greater than in younger population.

The consequences are sever and could potentially disrupt numerous biochemical processes happening within our body, e.g., energy production, cellular growth and repair mechanisms, disruption to neurotransmitter systems that are vital for brain communication with muscles, organs, and the autonomic nervous system and movements in general, functioning of the central nervous system, etc. Proper and effective working systems in our body is an absolute requirement for a healthy heart, healthy respiration, nutrient absorption and elimination. This not only is important for our physical existence but also for our cognitive and behavioural wellbeing. A comprehensive report published in 2018 by Dr. Celia Wilkinson, *Older Australians: Trends and Impacts of Alcohol and Other Drug Use*, provided a critical insight into substance abuse trends among older Australians. The report is detailed and well-referenced, and several key findings are presented here. In the case of alcohol use or abuse:

- In 2016, nearly 1 in 4 males (24.3%) and 7.7% of females aged 65–74 consumed more than two standard drinks per day on average.
- Over 20.9% of males and 4.6% of females in the same group consumed more than four standard drinks per day at least monthly, though not weekly.
- Among Indigenous Australians aged 55 and over (2015), 19% of males and 4.7% of females exceeded the two-standard-drink guideline.

The reasons behind alcohol use or over use in later life vary. Early-onset users often continue long-standing patterns of consumption, whereas late-onset users may turn to alcohol in response to grief, loneliness, chronic pain, retirement, or emotional distress. For many older adults, alcohol provides a sense of social connection or emotional relief. However, what begins as a coping mechanism may become a serious health risk, particularly when combined with medications or pre-existing conditions. Although research is limited in the case of illicit drugs, the data available suggests that illicit drug use is also present and increasing among older Australians:

- In 2016, 6.3% of Australians aged 65 and over reported using an illicit drug in the past year, up from 3.9% in 2001.
- Cannabis use in men aged 65+ more than doubled from 0.6% to 1.3%, while use in women increased fivefold (from 0.1% to 0.5%).
- Among Australians aged 55 and older, 0.2% reported recent use of cocaine, methamphetamine, or ecstasy.

The pattern of drug use reflects those reported with alcohol use; the early-onset users may maintain lifelong habits, whereas late-onset users may be influenced by loss, trauma, or new relationships, especially where partners are current users. For some, the use is habitual or perceived as unremarkable. For others, it's situational and reactive. Misuse of prescription medications among the elderly is a growing yet considered an under-recognised issue:

- In 2016, 4.9% of women and 4.7% of men aged 65 and older reported non-medical use of pharmaceuticals.
- Pharmaceutical misuse was more prevalent in this group than the combined use of cannabis, cocaine, methamphetamines, and ecstasy.

Interestingly, most elderly adults do not misuse prescription medications to achieve a high. Rather, they often attempt to extend or amplify the original therapeutic effects of the medication, especially when managing chronic conditions such as pain, anxiety, or insomnia, hoping that misuse or overuse may have a faster response onset. This pattern, however, can lead to unintended dependence and longer-term use which often goes medically un-noticed with certain consequences. With continued improvements in medicine, institutionalized age-care the current generation of older Australians are much healthier and living longer than ever before than previous generations.

4. Infections and cognitive decline:

There is growing evidence that infections can contribute to cognitive impairment in older adults. Research suggests that certain infections may trigger or accelerate cognitive decline, and in some cases, this decline may be reversed once the infection is controlled. However, in vulnerable individuals particularly those with pre-existing conditions, e.g., cognitive deficits or dementia such infections may exacerbate long-term neurological damage. According to the Alzheimer's Society UK, infections such as herpes simplex, pneumonia, syphilis, Lyme disease, and periodontal (gum) disease have been associated with an increased risk of dementia and cognitive impairment (*Alzheimer's Society UK, 2023*). Lyme disease is a bacterial infection caused by tick bites. Recent studies also indicate that COVID-19 may have a significant impact on cognitive function. In a 2023 study published in the *Journal of Clinical Medicine,* it is reported that cognitive decline post-COVID-19 was more pronounced in elderly individuals, particularly those with pre-existing dementia or other neurodegenerative conditions (J Clin Med. 2023 Mar; 12(5):1845).

5. De-generation of neurones and neurodegenerative conditions:

This occurs when our brain nerve cells are impaired and dying causing a disruption in the neuron communication with other parts of the body such as movements and memory functions (e.g., motor neuron disease, Parkinsonism, Alzheimer's disease, etc.). This is a severe health issue in the elderly population and also affects our central and peripheral nervous systems (CNS and PNS). Neurodegenerative conditions have a very wide health implications, it is estimated that there are around 50 million sufferers in the world; in US alone there are 7-8 million and in Australia, between 1-1.5 million people are regular sufferers. This figure is likely to increase annually with the increase in the ageing population.

Readers interested in this subject may check out the following reference (*my.clevelandclinic.org/health/diseases/24976-neurodegenerative-diseases*). In up-coming nations e.g. in India the number of people suffering from dementia is estimated to be 3 million and rising. Neurodegenerative conditions are irreversible and currently there are no cures, but certain treatments are available to relieve some of the symptoms.

6. Mild cognitive impairment (MCI):

Generally MCI is a mild form of dementia and can be helped with proper healthcare medication and good nutrition. If not arrested and proper treatment regime is activated at the onset of the condition then patients can drift into dementia progressively and accelerate with advancing age. There are several symptoms that we all should be aware of, few of them are,

Systemic disorders and/or impairments_

As we age our ability to digest and metabolism decreases. Ingested food/ medicines etc. need to be firstly digested in order to extract the benefit that the ingested food offers.

Here are the Basic Systemic Biochemical steps:

Generally, there are 5 basic systemic biochemical steps which control or regulate our biochemical existence. Most of us will agree that our body needs energy for its continued existence. The food we ingest is the only fuel source which goes through several biochemical processes ending in the production of energy which is the driving force for all our bodily function which keeps us alive for example our breathing, sleeping, and metabolic functions are all energy-dependent. So let us see the fate of foods we eat in order to provide us with the all-important energy.

The schematic diagramme presented will, I hope simplify the complex procedures that are happening in the body. The important point to note is that the effectiveness and efficiency of each of these fundamental steps are highly dependent on our food source and the processing steps. If the quality of food ingested is not of a basic standard of requirement then the processing steps suffer to deliver the results. For example, if the food supplied is high in say fats and oils, sugar or salt, too much of carbohydrate and not enough of nutrient content or nutritional value then our digestion suffers which results in slow or ineffective absorption which in turn will cause lack of tissue or cellular deposit of nutrient due to inadequate circulation processes. So, our cells will be deprived of nutrition resulting in cell death or inefficient cellular function causing low energy production and our biochemical existence suffers. So, it is important to have a balanced mix of the five categories of food groups in our diet.

5 basic Systemic Biochemical steps

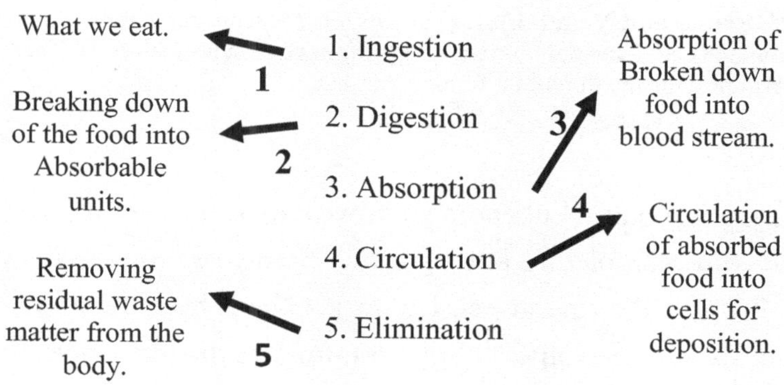

If the organs participating in each of the systems are impaired or functionally weak then dysfunction or inadequate performance in any of the five biochemical steps can manifest into a biochemical condition leading from mild to serious consequences in patient's general health and well-being and in seniors it may also affect the rate of cognitive decline.

Incorporating each group in appropriate proportions helps maintain nutritional adequacy and dietary variety. So, what are the 5 basic food groups that we should try to incorporate in our daily dietary intake? Food should be enjoyed and so to break the monotony of our dietary habits we should include all five food groups in a balanced and tasteful portions.

5 Food Categories	Nutritional Source

1. **Carbohydrates:** Carbohydrates are a good source of fibres, starch and sugars which are body's main fuel. They also provide small amounts of vitamins.

2. **Fats, Oils and Proteins:** Fats provide most energy to our body when needed; Proteins are rich in amino acids which are the building blocks of our body.

3. **Cereals, Nuts and Legumes:** This group of food is a good source of protein, healthy fats, fibre, vitamins and minerals.

4. **Milk and Dairy:** Dairy products are made from milk and are a rich sources of Calcium, Magnesium, Zinc, Iodine, Phosphorous, Vitamins A, D and B12 and many other micronutrients for our growth and well-being.

5. **Fruits and Vegetables:** Oxidants, phytochemicals, vitamins and minerals are essential nutrient groups from vegetables and fruits. They also provide the important fibre in our diets.

Ageing is a natural phenomenon; we are born to get old and finally pass-on, thus completing our life-cycle. Some age quicker than others and it is up to the care givers, law makers, and health professionals to factor in the old age vulnerabilities to minimize the incidences of misuse overuse of alcohol, illicit drugs, and prescription items.

Chapter 4

AGE RELATED ANATOMICAL PHYSIOLOGICAL CHANGES AND RELATED HEALTH IMPAIRMENTS

"Age is a timeless journey of maturation—an evolution that gently mellows with time."

– Jay Das ... 2024

Age-related health impairments

are not uncommon, and we are not just talking about the cuts and bruises that we all suffer on a regular basis; some go through this more regularly than others.

Health conditions associated with ageing that we seniors should be concerned about in my summation can be categorised into 3 main areas not necessarily in any particular order:

1. Psychological
2. Physiological
3. Systemic

Psychological issues dealing with mental health, cognitive functions and personal awareness are common in most elderly people. There may be myriads of reasons why elderly people suffer from depression, anxiety, fear anger and other emotional stress-related conditions. Each case must be assessed on individual circumstances and intervened accordingly.

Physiological issues concerning the decline in anatomical functions resulting from the ageing of our organs Systemic impairments which may affect our bodily functions such as digestive, circulation, respiratory, elimination systems, etc., which could also be linked with the dysfunction of various organs associated with these systems. I have also included the sensory issues of touch, smell, hearing, taste, etc. Our ageing process has many positives if we can manage it with a self-awareness input but it also comes with certain inevitable negatives. Our organs age with us causing all sorts of health problems which we need to be aware of at the earliest warning signs and start taking some preventive action to keep these health conditions away as long as we can. This can only be achieved if we can improve our self-awareness and get timely professional help. Many of us in our senior years are embarrassed to seek help and leave it until it is too serious to live with. But, by that time it really be too late. The key word here is to get timely intervention and give your health a fighting chance to add to a few more good years that your life can offer.

Psychological: Cognitive impairment and mental health issues have been discussed in the previous chapter at a brief but awareness level. According to Mayo Clinic in America, there are some basic warning signs that we in our senior years should take note of (*Ref: www.mayoclinic.org/diseases-conditions/mental-illness/symptoms-causes/syc-20374968*).

Sometimes we are so engrossed in our sufferings that it becomes practically difficult to manage self-awareness in this condition so the responsibility falls on to our partners, peer group and the people close to us to intervene and take appropriate action. Some of the early warning signs which if not intervened at the right time could manifest into full-blown mental issues.

- Mood changes with frequent highs and lows
- Alcohol and drug dependency
- Detachment from regular friends and social activities
- Dazed and in a state of confusion and loss of rationality
- Changes in eating habits and weight loss symptoms
- Feeling sad and lonely even though there is support available
- Tiredness, loss of energy and irregular sleep patterns
- Social fear, shyness and withdrawal tendencies
- In extreme cases violence and suicidal tendencies

Any sign or symptoms which seem unusual and not normal behaviour could point out that there is something wrong and trigger for intervention. **Physiological:** Our ageing process is characterised by our steep decline in biological functions as compared to when we were young adults. Ageing organs and systemic deficiencies put a lot of load and stress on our metabolisms and the functioning of various systems which require a bunch of organs pertaining to that system to work in unison to provide the best possible outcome. If one or more organs fail to deliver then physiological efficiencies are greatly reduced, resulting in a systemic breakdown or organ failure which results in a disease state requiring urgent medical intervention. Although this may not happen suddenly and warning signs are critical to watch out for. During my studies and research, I found several important points for consideration on age-related physiological disorders, their basic reasons and their health implications. It is never easy to write a thesis or treaties on any subject let alone human nature and health but it has become a bit easier for me being a senior citizen myself, as I still have the capability of analysing data and reviews on this subject and put pen to paper and hopefully make it interesting reading. Considering physiology and age it seems to me that as far as anatomy is concerned there are four important organs which need to be understood and maintained for wear and tear. These four organs can cause the bulk of health conditions therefore I consider these to be of significance. **Our heart** is the major organ of our Circulatory System and works like a pump. To understand the details of its workings it will require some understanding of the anatomy of our heart. For our general awareness I will keep it simple but in reality it is more complex. With years of pumping and not much maintenance its efficiency diminishes resulting in the decrease in cardiac output, it is another way of saying that with age our heart pumps less blood. This has a serious consequences on our blood pressure and related physiological issues. There is also wear and tear of the blood vessels which need to be considered. Anatomically our heart has 4 chambers or cavities; two on the right side and two on the left side. The working of our heart can be simply represented by the following schematic diagramme.

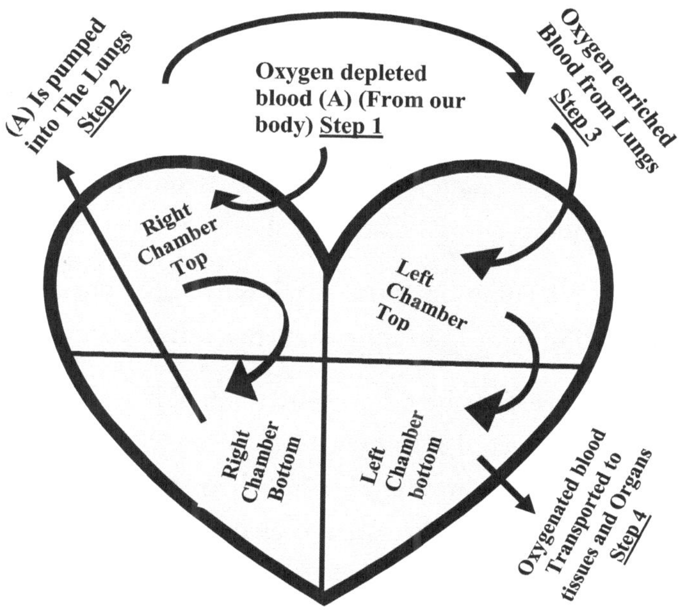

Step 1: Oxygen-depleted blood (A) from our body enters the top right chamber of the heart also called the right atrium. **Step 2:** The oxygen-depleted blood from the right atrium then is pumped into the bottom right chamber (the right ventricle) from there the blood is pumped into our Lungs to be oxygenated.

Step 3: The Oxygen enriched blood is then pumped into the top left chamber of the heart (the left atrium). **Step 4:** Blood from the left atrium is then pumped into the bottom left chamber (left ventricle) via the aortic valve and circulated into the whole body.

This pump action of the heart is a critical function for the body because the circulating blood deposits the nutrients and the Oxygen into various cells and tissues for our organs to live and function normally. Any dysfunction of the heart's pumping action can cause insufficient nutrients and Oxygen to reach our brain and other organs causing them to starve and become dysfunctional and may cause eventual death.

There can be several diseases of the circulatory system that we are likely to encounter as we age. Many of these are caused by our heart which is the primary organ and undergoes a sequence of wear and tear due to its continuous efforts to keep us alive.

Here are some common issues that we need to consider and which also act as warning signs indicating immediate medical intervention.

Blood pressure: Our blood pressure is a highly regulated parameter. It is the measure which determines the force by which the heart pumps our blood through the arteries. Too much or too little force can lead to inefficient and insufficient carriage of nutrients, oxygen and several components in the blood to various tissues of our body. Our blood pressure is the collective force applied by passage of blood not just by the main arteries but also by smaller blood vessels, e.g., capillaries as well. So, too much blood pressure will cause damage to the integrity of such blood vessels.

The measurement of our blood pressure is quite critical and is measured at two points. First, the pressure point at the start of heart beat, this is the top reading and called ***systolic*** blood pressure. The second point is the pressure at rest in between heartbeats, this is called **diastolic** blood pressure.

Our blood pressure is expressed by putting these two numbers together **systolic over diastolic** blood pressure**.** Ideally, our systolic blood pressure reading should be close to 120 and the diastolic around 80. An ideal blood pressure should read 120/80 mmHg. The gauge which reads the blood pressure is called **Sphygmomanometer** and reads the blood pressure is expressed in millimetres of mercury (mmHg).

As we age this blood pressure reading can fluctuate and change and may be characteristics of your age health condition and other factors such as your exercise and movement regime, dietary habits and lifestyle. Usually, your healthcare professional will set a limit to the upper (systolic) parameter for regular monitoring. The diastolic reading is less critical but again requires regular monitoring which your doctor will set a limit to.

Blood pressure can fluctuate in elderly people due to several reasons.

Our blood vessels carrying continuous blood flow can get fragile, they may become stiffer and lose flexibility also, may also cause friction and develop resistivity towards a smooth flow of blood which is essential for consistent blood pressure and flow.

A consistent flow of blood helps to carry toxins and waste matters for our liver and kidneys to process and eliminate. High blood pressure can damage our kidneys and therefore reduces the efficiency of the elimination process.

Due to excessive dietary fats, fatty and cholesterol deposits may cause blood vessels (arteries) to clog up. This along with excessive free calcium circulating in the blood which remains unabsorbed by our cells and tissues has nowhere to go but combines with excess fats and cholesterol to form deadly combinations and deposits in and around the arteries and logging them. These plaques formed are quite difficult to remove restricting the blood flow and causing hardening of the arteries and other blood vessels. This is known as Atherosclerosis and is one of the reasons for high blood pressure in elderly people and in general people with high fatty diets.

Other common causes of high blood pressure are:

Not drinking enough water causes the blood to become thicker than normal causing the heart to overwork and use extra effort to push the blood through the blood vessels.

Effect of certain medications, e.g., certain over-the-counter pain killers, medications which have blood-thinning effect (Aspirin), diuretics which cause water to be eliminated from the body and certain herbs. It is therefore important that before taking any medication and supplements on a regular and prolonged basis elderly citizens must consult their medical professionals.

Other common lifestyle causes are

- Obesity
- Lack of movement and physical activities,
- High-fatty diet and high salt intake,
- High stress and anxiety suffers
- Genetic and hereditary traits.
- Diabetes
- Excessive smoking and alcohol use

Positive changes in lifestyle can drastically help balance blood pressure and improve circulation.

Heart failure means that the heart is not pumping blood around the body as efficiently as it should. It can lead to fatigue, shortness of breath, and coughing. These signs can also be taken as warning signs and must be checked out for root cause.

A stroke can happen when one of the vessels that lead to the brain either becomes blocked by a blood clot or bursts. This stops blood flow and prevents oxygen from getting to the brain.

It is estimated that around 1.28 billion of global population aged 30-79 years suffer from hypertension, most of whom are from poorer countries. Half of the suffering population is not even aware of this condition and many still do not have a regular blood pressure check (*Ref: www.who.int/news-room/fact-sheets/detail/hypertension*). Blood pressure if not diagnosed and treated, can, lead to serious conditions such as heart disease, stroke, kidney impairment, eye problems and many other health conditions. Some of these conditions in the elderly population can be very serious and may become chronic throughout their life. According to the centres for Disease Control and Prevention (CDC) in US alone, about 70% of the adult population 65 years and older have high blood pressure (Hypertension) and may not even know about it. In Australia, this number could be as high as 40% in the age group 65-74 years

(*Ref: www.aihw.gov.au/reports/older-people/olderaustralians/contents/health/health-risk-factors*)

Here are some interesting facts about our heart worth noting.

- Our heart is a pump which continuously pumps around 7.5 litres of blood every day for 80-85 years depending on a person's longevity.
- Heart can continue beating up to 4-6 hours after it has been detached from the body.
- Blue whales have the largest heart of any mammal approx. 450kg; compared to the human heart which weighs less than 500g.
- Reducing stress and anxiety is good for the heart and laughter is the best medicine and boosts our immunity.
- A woman's heart beats slightly faster than a man's heart.
- Is There a Better Time of Day to Have a Heart Attack? Yes there is. Most heart attacks happen on a Monday (*Ref: Circulation Research. 2010; 106:430–431*), so watch out and keep your heart safe especially on Mondays.
- The earliest heart disease was found in a 3,500 years old Egyptian mummy.
- Dr. Christiaan Barnard a South African Cardiac Surgeon with his team, performed the world's first human-to-human heart transplant

operation on 3 December 1967. He was nominated for Nobel Prize in physiology in 1968 but unfortunately missed out.

The next organ to consider is our lungs situated on each side of our trachea or the windpipe connected via the bronchi which provides air we breathe in to the lungs. They are part of our Respiratory System.

Simplified Lung anatomy (Ref: modified from https://en.wikipedia.org/wiki/Lung)

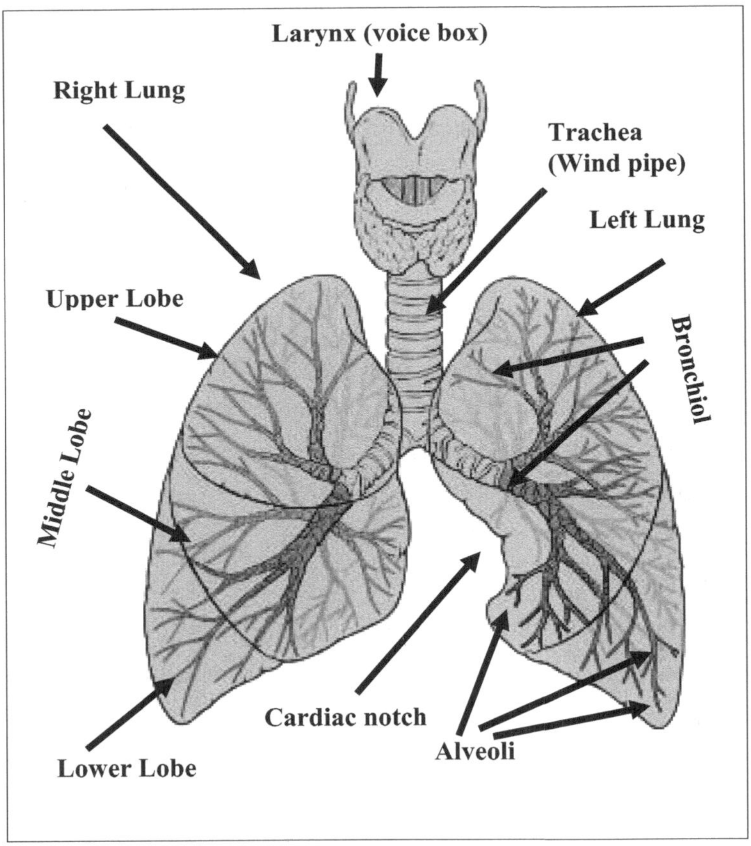

Our lungs provide a very important service to our body. The basic unit of our tissues and organs, the cells and cellular structure require oxygen to sustain life and without the availability oxygen our survival would not be possible. Our lungs and other components of the respiratory system are entrusted to perform the breathing in of the oxygen-enriched air into the lungs and to carry it through to our heart which is then transported into each and every cell of our body where the gas exchange occurs; oxygen is deposited and the waste gas primarily carbon dioxide is removed from the lungs when we exhale.

There are several disease states when our lungs may show signs of functional deficiencies which could be life-threatening if not addressed and proper care regimen is not put in place. Some of these diseases are more prevalent as we age and also erratic lifestyle such as excessive smoking, alcohol and drug abuse and can also be environmental.

Asthma: It is a respiratory condition which causes narrowing of our airways leading to our lungs and triggers breathing difficulties, coughing and wheezing, shortness of breath and several breathing difficulty episodes. This can happen due to excess mucus accumulating in the windpipe and other areas of lungs causing a decrease in the lung capacity. Pollution and allergens are also a primary cause of Asthma. In most people asthma is manageable by a structured care plan but in others it can be a major health issue which severely affects their daily routine.

Pneumonia: Is a condition when the air sacs also called the alveoli in the lungs get infected causing contaminated fluid build-up. It can be bacterial, viral and fungal in nature and therefore is a difficult disease to tackle in elderly people with weak immunity. It may affect one or both lungs causing a cough bringing out a lot of phlegm and mucus with pus and is generally associated with temperature, a condition where a patient shivers and has breathing problems. If not treated at the onset of the symptoms it could become serious and even life-threatening.

Allergy: Seasonal allergies and lung diseases have a special relationship. Almost all of the common lung diseases we succumb to are triggered by some form of allergic response. These allergic responses are manifestations of very common lung conditions such as asthma, allergic bronchitis, and breathing difficulties ranging from simple breathing issues to wheezing and even coughing. Seasonal allergies are mainly caused by exposure to pollen and other vegetation fragments floating in the air and getting into our airways through the nose eventually affecting our lungs. Some of the lung diseases are more commonly known as Cystic fibrosis, Allergic Rhinitis commonly known as hay fever, chronic obstructive pulmonary disease (COPD) and Chronic respiratory diseases (CRDs) and many more; big names indeed yet to sensitive persons with weaker immunity like we seniors these diseases can be a nightmare during Autumn and Spring.

Obesity: Increased weight leading to obesity and BMI as a measure of obesity has a significant effect on the aged population. Excess weight per square meter body surface can exert excessive pressure on the chest cavity housing several of our vital organs causing a restrictive functional impairment in those organs. The major complications can be in the area of the respiratory system, cardiac function and to a certain degree the liver. However, more restrictive pressure is exerted on our lungs and heart due to the organ's mechanical action e.g. Lungs inflate and deflate while heart muscles expand and contract causing some restrictive force on the chest cavity. This can cause a weakness on the respiratory muscle strength and the pericardium of the heart which is a protective outer membrane of the heart offering protection to the heart from friction and mechanical pressure caused by nearby internal body structures.

Cystic Fibrosis: Cystic Fibrosis (CF) is a genetic disease which affects several organs of our body due to an overproduction of sticky viscous mucus in various organs causing a severe impairment in the functionality of the organ. In the Lungs it causes excess mucus to choke the airways with severe breathing difficulties and lung damage. Often these mucus deposits can harden up into a fibrous layer which is difficult to dislodge and turns into a life-threatening situation with reduced life expectancy.

The mucus deposit offers an ideal breeding environment for bacterial and fungal growth and therefore CF sufferers are very prone to developing secondary infections and cause inflammation which can lead to respiratory failure ending in a premature death.

Testing our own lung functions on a regular basis can be the first warning step to self-assessment, and should alert suffers to seek medical assistance at the first warning trigger. A report should be kept for your professional career.

One of the simplest home hand-held device is the **Peak Flow meter** (PFM) and measures the strength of the breath to measure the force of the expiration of the air out of the lung. The procedure of exhaling must be uniform for the reading to be consistent and meaningful. Follow the simple technique of taking a deep breath, then using the blow-piece of the device to your mouth to create a seal so no air can escape when blowing as hard but in a consistent manner. The reading should be indicated on the graduated scale. Repeat the procedure at least a couple of more times, each time before blowing set the reading indicator to zero or start point. Relax for a few seconds, take a deep breath and then blow in one continuous expiration or breathe out. The maximum reading should be recorded with date and time. The result is typically expressed as litres per minute or as L/min.

Before you engage in self-assessment please check with your professional health care provider for recommendation of a PFM to suite your general health and age. The Caregiver should also be able to recommend the optimal time for your daily measurement and could also show you the proper use of the device and record keeping.

Some interesting facts about our lungs:

- Our lungs on either side of the trachea are not symmetrical. Lung on the left-hand side is slightly smaller than on the right side.
- We inhale about 11-15 thousand litres of air per day of which around 20% (about 2500 Litres) is oxygen.
- We inhale about 11-15 Thousand litres of air per day of which around 20% (about 2500 Litres) is oxygen.
- In each breath we breathe in about 0.5 litres of air.
- We exhale a similar quantity of air of which about 15% is oxygen.
- Our body uses only 5% of oxygen from the air we breathe in, the rest is exhaled with the air we breathe out.
- Our lungs just by breathing out eliminates 70% of the wastes mainly in the form of carbon-di-oxide gas.
- Interesting question; can we live with only one lung? Yes, we can, but with restrictions and some limitations. Many people in the world live as normal life as possible with only one lung.
- Our lungs always retain around 1 litre of air irrespective of how we breathe out, otherwise our lungs will collapse. Due to this air retention, our lungs are the only organ which can float in water.
- Adult lung capacity is around 5L of air. Lung capacity decreases greatly as we age.
- Adults lose around 17-18mL of water every hour when they exhale. This amounts to around 250mL of water a day.
- Lungs are also important for our body temperature regulation, support our sense of smell and speech.

Our Lungs are therefore a very vital organ and is like a fuel source for our body extracting energy source (Oxygen) from external raw material, the air. Next organ that deserves mention is **our Kidneys**. These smaller organs are around 12 cm in length (5 inches in the old scale) and weighs around 150g each. In females, the kidneys are slightly smaller. Our left kidney is usually slightly larger than the right kidney. The size of the kidney is also dependent on our body structure such as our height, body weight, gender and age. They are like bean shaped and located on either side of our spine at the back of our stomach. You must have heard and seen the red kidney beans and resemble our kidneys very closely only that they are much smaller in dimension. Our kidneys perform many important functions, let's itemise some, without these vital functions our survival could be at stake. Our kidneys **filter our blood**; this is their primary function. In doing so, they remove the waste and deposit it into our bladder via the tubes called **Ureter** for elimination as urine. They control our **electrolyte balance** so that the intra-cellular (inside of a cell) and the extra-cellular (outside of a cell) osmotic pressure across the cell membrane are at a perfect balance so that our cells will maintain structural integrity and perform optimally to carry oxygen and nutrients to all the parts of our body. They control our **blood pH** to a targeted pH range of 7.35 – 7.45 under normal healthy conditions. This is done by controlling the release or re-absorption of bicarbonate (HCO3-) and, or, the acidic ions (H+). Our kidneys also have an input in controlling our blood pressure. Our Kidneys **secrete several important biochemical** such as hormones, steroids etc. which are essential for our general health and well-being. For example the hormone **Renin** which is required for the regulation of our blood pressure; **Erythropoietin** is essential for the manufacture of red blood cells when required in our bone marrow where they are produced. Also, our adrenal glands which is situated at the top of the kidneys produce the steroidal hormone called Cortisol in response to our body's defence mechanism responding to stress and danger (flight or fight symptom). If our kidneys are not functioning adequately or are impaired due to some diseases, then the following common problems can be noticed and could manifest as moderate to severe health care alerts; medical intervention becomes critical. **Chronic and acute renal failure:** These are both symptoms of moderate to severe kidney failure and can happen if the kidneys have not been functioning due to dehydration, urinary tract blockages, blood pressure fluctuations, the effect of medication, allergy and several other health conditions. This condition can be reversed with proper medical intervention. **Kidney stones:** Often you hear the condition where stones are formed in the kidney and urinary tract. This is caused by mineral deposits accumulating over time to form a hard stone-like formation of different sizes. These stones can move down the urinary tract in the ureters and get lodged into the bladder and cause blockages and difficulty in urination. The result is severe sharp pain, nausea and vomiting, shivers with temperature and often blood in the urine. **Polycystic kidney disease:** This is caused by the formation of large cysts and growth in both kidneys and is known to be a genetic condition. This causes the kidney functions to diminish markedly. It is believed that high blood pressure and diabetes could be the common causes.

Diabetic nephropathy: This is another common kidney disease that you may have heard of. This is caused due to high blood sugar content which slowly builds up and progressively damages the kidneys. Proteinuria may develop causing protein to escape into the urine.

There are several other common kidney and bladder issues with ageing which require a lot of consideration.

Urinary incontinence is the inability to hold urination, also, urinary retention where the bladder is never completely empty even though urine may have been passed freely. This leftover urine in the bladder causes casual or frequent dribbling of urine and may soil the clothing unless adequate protection has been applied with the underclothing.

Urinary tract infection (UTI): is as the name suggests, a bacterial infection in any part of the urinary tract consisting mainly of the kidneys, ureters, bladder and urethra. A picture of our urinary system is presented below and is gratefully referenced from Hopkins Medicine (*Ref:*

www.hopkinsmedicine.org/health/wellness-and prevention /an atomy-of-the-urinary-system). Women are more at risk than men and the infection can be more noticed in the lower urinary tract. The infection can cause pain and irritation and if not treated using appropriate antibiotic medication at the onset of the infection serious health issues can develop. Proper sanitation and hygiene must be practised to protect against UTI.

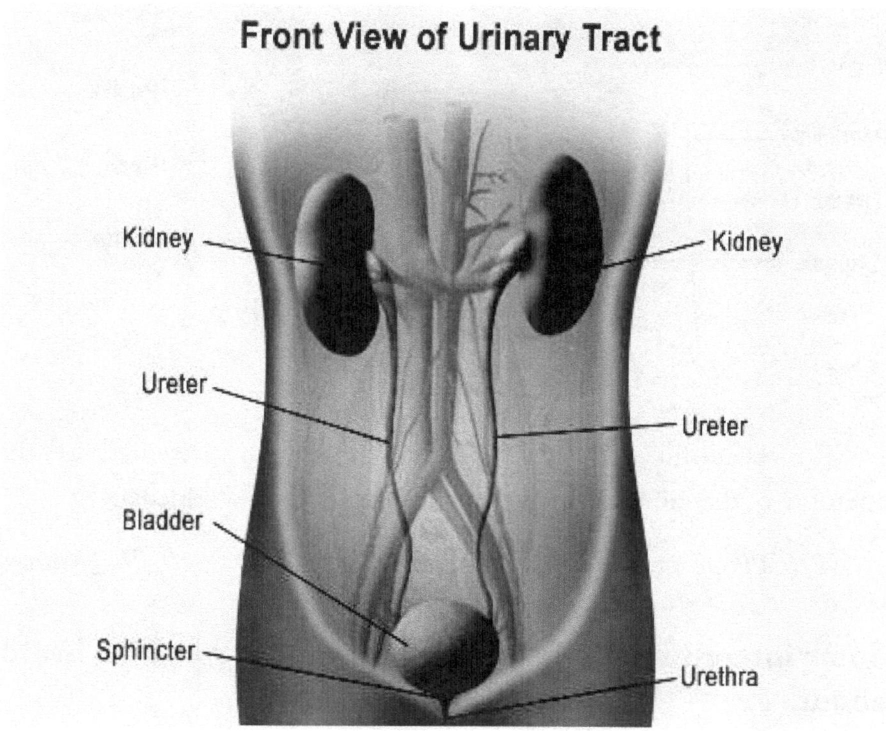

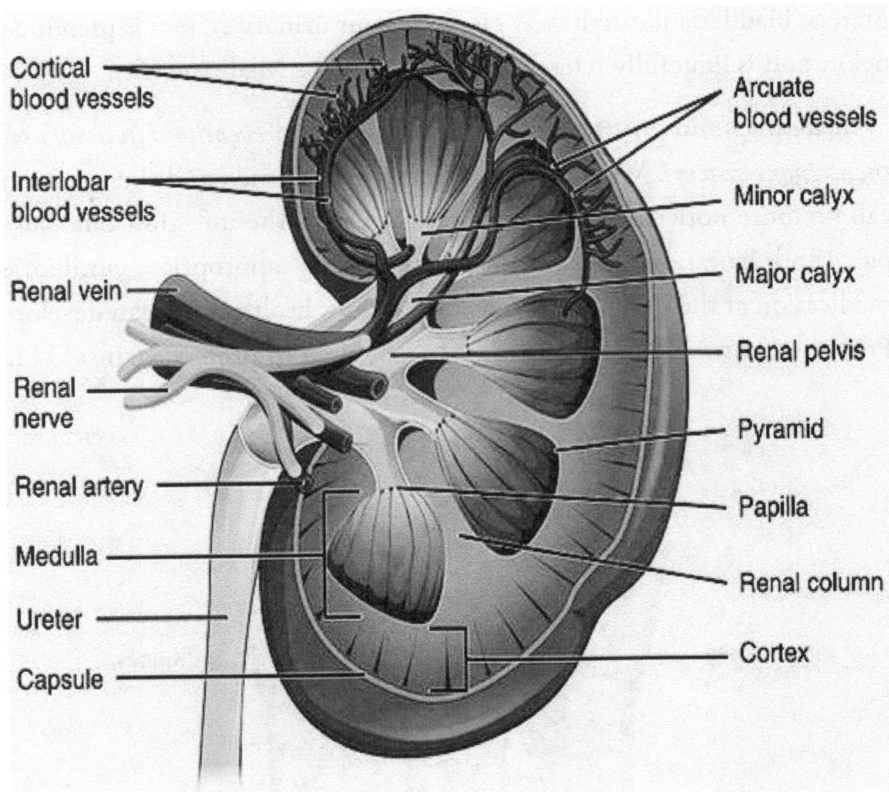

This beautiful and well-described illustration presented of the anatomy of the kidney is gratefully referenced from Wikipedia.

(Ref: Wikipedia https://en.wikipedia.org "wiki "File:2610_The_Kidney)

Some interesting kidney facts that you may not have heard about.

- It is very rare incidence that a few people are born with only one kidney and even fewer with three kidneys, yet they are known to live a healthy and active life.

- Normally we have two kidneys, but it is possible to live a healthy life with only one functional kidney. Hence, kidney donation is not uncommon.
- In many instances some of us have only 10% of the kidneys functioning and yet we can lead a normal life.
- Our functioning kidneys filter around 200 Litres of blood every day. This equates to about the entire volume of blood in an adult body passing through our kidneys 40 times daily.
- Our right kidney is slightly smaller and positioned little bit lower than left kidney. This asymmetry is to accommodate our liver which a larger organ and sits predominantly in the right side of our body.
- The largest kidney stone ever recorded weighed around 1.1kg and in shaped like a coconut.
- The earliest recording (in Egyptian Papyrus) about our kidneys dates back to 3500 years.
- World's first kidney transplant attempt was in Ukraine (1933) by Dr. Yuri Voronoy. Unfortunately, it was not successful.
- The first successful kidney transplant was in 1954 in Boston USA by Dr. Joseph E. Smith.

Although our kidneys are very resilient, changes do occur with ageing. Around the age of 50 we start losing some of the kidney functions but as mentioned earlier to normal healthy people it does not matter too much.

When we consider our major organs we cannot go past **our Liver**. It is possibly the least glamourous organ in our anatomy yet vital which we cannot do without. Although all our body parts in one way or another vital to our health and well-being, I feel the liver deserves a lot of praise and consideration.

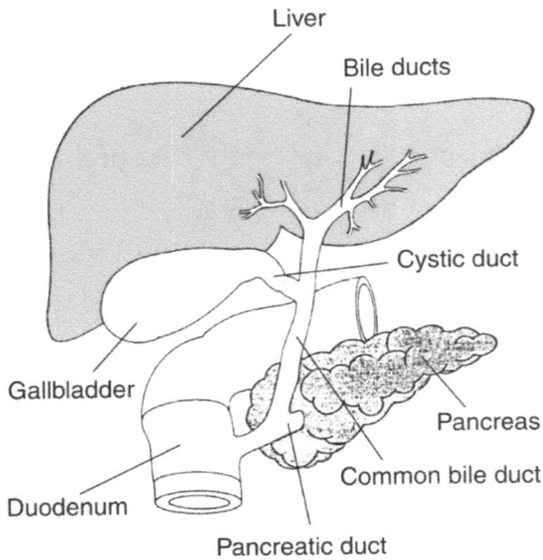

A drawing of the biliary system showing the liver, gallbladder, pancreas, duodenum, bile ducts, cystic duct, common bile duct, and pancreatic duct labelled (Referenced with sincere gratefulness to National Institute of Diabetes and Digestive and Kidney Diseases, National Institute of Health).

Our liver is the largest and heaviest internal organ in our body. Adult liver weighs around 1500g (average weight) but can weigh as much as 1700g. It sits under the rib cage on the right-hand side just under the stomach.

Our liver is an amazing and forgiving organ and performs many significant functions to sustain our life; some of those vital functions are listed below.

- The liver filters our blood and neutralizes externally introduced toxins such as preservatives, environmentally hazardous chemicals, harmful ingredients resulting from the breakdown of foodstuff and medicinal products we intake and also effects of alcohol, drug and smoking abuses and many more to keep us healthy.

- It produces bile to help digest fats, proteins and oils from our foods.
- Cholesterol which we all are familiar with is produced in our liver and circulated in all cells in our body as it is an integral constituent of our cell walls.
- Our Liver metabolizes the drug molecules we take in as medication and neutralizes the harmful and toxic metabolites (by products) that are left over after the good bits from the medicines are used up.
- Liver also makes most of the proteins circulating in our blood particularly albumin which is one of the marker for liver health.
- The liver also activates several endocrine system hormones, and manufactures a few e.g. Angiotensinogen which is a part of the Sodium and potassium regulatory system, Thrombopoietin a hormone also produced in the liver and is responsible for the regulation of the platelets in the blood and Hepcidin a hormone produced in the liver and activates Ferro protein for the regulation and utilization of iron in the circulating blood.
- Liver also manufactures and activates several important enzymatic systems within our body. For example, the most common ones with which many of us are familiar with are:

Alkaline phosphatase (ALP).
Alanine transaminase (ALT).
Aspartate transaminase (AST).
Gamma-glutamyl transferase (GGT).

Some of these appear as markers for liver health when we get our blood tested.

What are enzymes? Ok, for your simple understanding enzymes are bioactive protein molecules which catalyse, meaning speed up numerous biochemical reactions being performed every moment within our body. These enzymes are important for our digestive system, organ functions, part take in various biosynthesis producing various molecular systems providing energy to our cells for their efficient functioning and many other activities.

Like enzymes, hormones are also protein molecules but they can also be steroids. These act as bio-chemical messengers which are important in the functioning of body by conveying messages. Our endocrine glandular system produces different hormones which activate many endocrine network functions as described later in this chapter.

Apart from performing a myriad of body of which only a few as mentioned above it can regenerate itself into a perfectly working organ. There is no artificial machine yet invented that can mimic all of our body functions that our liver performs on a daily basis. It is not a matter of only a few bodily functions but talking about around 500 separate functions that our liver is entrusted to perform on a daily basis.

Alcohol, drug abuse and cigarette smoking are all injurious to our liver health.

A healthy liver can filter about 1.7 Litres of blood every minute, and at any given moment liver can hold up to 15% of our entire volume of blood.

During pregnancy and childbirth the liver can expand in size and weight to cater for the additional requirements in a mother to compensate for excess metabolism and hormonal balance.

The regeneration of the liver is something of a miracle. In 1989 a slice of adult liver was transplanted into a child resulting in both patients developing perfectly normal livers. Since then many partial liver transplantation has been successful so long as at least 25% of the healthy liver is left in the donor to regenerate.

The first successful liver transplant was carried out by Dr. Thomas E. Starzi in 1967 at the University of Colorado in Denver, his patient survived for more than a year longest since any previous transplant recipient.

In ancient times liver was seen to be the centre of our soul and all forms of emotional and mental activities.

It is also believed that the ancient Mesopotamians constructed clay liver models to study liver anatomy as early as 2000 BC.

(*Reference: History of liver anatomy: Mesopotamian liver clay models (HPB (Oxford). 2013 Apr; 15(4): 322–323*).

Model ME92668, held at the Middle East Department of the British Museum, dates back to 2000BC (Fig 1 and 2)

(Figure 1: Visceral Surface of the Clay Model.)

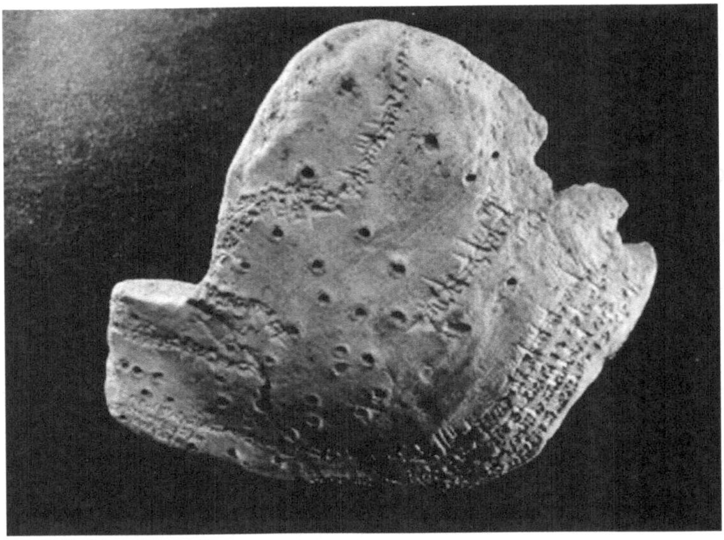

(Figure 2: Dia-phragmatic Surface of the Clay Model.)

We often talk about cells, tissues and organs and wonder what the relationship among them is. To understand this we need to look at our body as an entity made of the most fundamental building block *the atom.* Everything we see around is made of a collection of atoms. So, we human beings along with other living beings such as plants, insects, animals and all other organisms are composed of a combination of atoms arranged in the following sequence leading to the final stage.

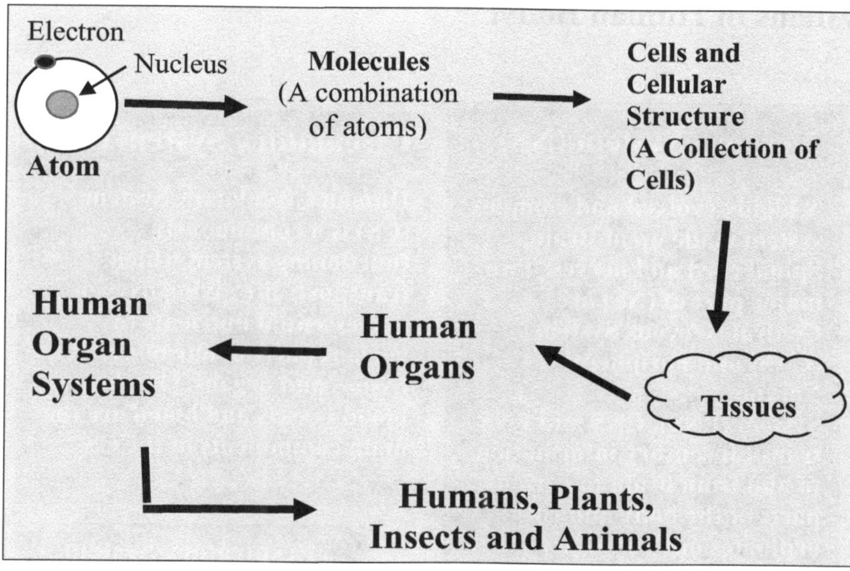

Interestingly enough, an atom is an in-organic entity, but a combination of special atoms give rise to organic beings such as us.

Systems in Human Body:

Nervous System (NS)

A highly evolved and complex system made up of Brain, Spinal cord and nerves. Two major part of (NS) are Central Nervous System (CNS) and Peripheral Nervous System (PNS). CNS and PNS transmit sensory information to and from brain to various parts of the body and co-ordinates our voluntary movements and several other activities.

Circulatory System (CS)

Human Circulatory System (CS) is a continuously functioning system which transports life giving oxygen and essential nutrients to various parts of our body, tissues and organs. Our heart, blood vessels and blood are the main components of the CS.

Respiratory System (RS)

Respiratory System consists of many organs of which lungs are the most important functional organ. Primary function of (RS) is to extract oxygen from the air we breathe in and flush out the toxins from our body through carbon dioxide as we breathe out.

Musculoskeletal System (MSS)

Our musculoskeletal system (MSS) is made up of bones, muscle, joints, tendons and other tissues which is very important for our body framework to keep it erect, firm and in balance. Weakness in (MSS) will cause a lack of support for our bodyweight, posture and free movement.

Digestive System (DS)

Our Digestive System (DS) is like a food processor for our body. Foods we eat is processed into smaller and more convenient forms for absorption into our system for transportation and deposited into our cell structure for conversion into our life sustaining energy.

Our human body has many systems that work perfectly in harmony to keep our body working and alive.

All the systems in the human body have specific functions which are carried out by specific organs of that particular system. All these organs must work in unison to achieve the desired outcome. If we consider our body to be a highly efficient factory, then following analogy may be applied to the workings of each system. **Nervous system** (NS): is the head office with Brain as the managing director. It co-ordinates and delegates sensory messages by transmitting signals via a team of neurons to and from various parts of organs and muscles to act accordingly. **Digestive system** (DS): is the guts of the factory where all the processing happens. **Respiratory and the circulatory systems**: is the utility departments supplying external energy as oxygen from the air we breathe in and internally the nutrients processed by the digestive system. No factory can work efficiently without an energy supply. **Musculoskeletal system** (MS): is the structure or the framework of the factory. If the factory is not supported by a solid foundation and firm structure then it may not survive for long. Occasional tender loving care (TLC) and maintenance is necessary for the performance and longevity of the factory. Besides the 5 systems as in the schematic diagramme there are another 5 systems worth mentioning are as follows.

- Endocrine system:
- Immune and lymphatic system:
- Integumentary system:
- Renal system / Urinary system:
- Reproductive system:

These additional 5 systems are equally important as the previous 5 and complement each other. All these systems make the human body functional, and like a perfectly functional factory timely maintenance is required to improve efficiency and longevity particularly as we start to age.

The 5 additional systems as I have mentioned are also important as they perform the following physiological roles.

Endocrine system: Our endocrine system primarily consists of several glands we are quite familiar with. The major glands of the endocrine system are the pancreas, Thyroid, Parathyroid, Adrenal, and Pituitary glands.

Starting with the **Pancreas** which is responsible for the production and release of hormone insulin which is essential for controlling our blood sugar levels. It plays a massive role in the disease state of Diabetes.

Our **Thyroid** gland is an important part of the endocrine system network. Among other things, it produces the hormone Thyroxine with which we all are familiar with. Almost 20% - 25% of the elderly people globally suffer from hypothyroidism. More prevalent in under-developed countries with a lack of iodine in their diets. Women are more affected than the male population with risk increasing over the age of 65 years.

Parathyroid glands collectively consists of 4 very small oval-shaped glands which excrete parathyroid hormones (PTH) that regulates and control calcium levels in the blood. The parathyroid hormone has several important biochemical processes that cannot be performed if there is a glandular impairment or under-functioning glands.

PTH assists in the absorption of calcium from foods ingested
Regulation of calcium by our kidneys during filtration of blood

Release of calcium from our bone tissues into blood stream if and when required.

PTH also instructs the kidneys to convert the less active form of vitamin D3 (25-hydroxyvitamin D3) to the active form (1, 25-hydroxyvitamin D3) for an efficient absorption of calcium from the intestine.

Adrenal glands shaped like pyramids sit on top of our kidneys. It is quite small in size about 5-7cm in length and 3cm in height. Female glands are slightly smaller. For some reason, the left gland is larger than the right.

Adrenal glands produce hormones which is involved in and controls our fight or flight response such as stress hormones, adrenaline etc. and also produces epinephrine and norepinephrine which are hormones responding to our stress situations.

Other hormones produced that are important are cortisol, sex hormones (like Oestrogens and Androgens), etc. Adrenal glands also produce cortisol a steroidal hormone that has several functions such as response to stress levels, glucose metabolism, blood pressure control, inflammation reduction and many more.

Adrenal glands are very important to our healthy life and life style. In general, adrenal hormones assist in regulating our immune system, our metabolism, blood pressure, stress responses and many other important physiological functions.

We next visit our **Thymus** glands which are situated between our lungs just above and in front of our heart. It is most active during our puberty then starts to shrink in size and loses its activities. Its activity is most important during the growing-up stage to optimize the body's autoimmunity and plays a vital role in our defensive network and is a part of our endocrine system network. Unlike most of our other glands and organs it has a larger size for more activity during our childhood and by the time we reach 70-75 years there is nothing significant left of this gland except the fatty tissues eminence of its past glory.

Testes (male gland) and **Ovaries** (female gland) are primary organs of our reproductive system and are responsible for producing male sperm and female eggs (ova).

Our brain houses 3 very important endocrine glands **Hypothalamus**, **Pituitary** and **Pineal** glands. All three are very important for our health and survival.

Hypothalamus is the largest of the three and is located at the base of our brain in close proximity to the Pituitary gland. The name comes from the Greek word meaning "under chamber" as per the location of the gland. The most important function of the hypothalamus is to keep in a state of homeostasis, which means to bring the body to a state of equilibrium where all the chemical and physical functions of the body are maintained in a good working order. A few of the important functions of the hypothalamus gland is highlighted below.

It controls and manages our hormone system.

It controls our basic appetite, emotional responses, sexual behaviour or urges.

It also has a major role in controlling our body temperature and blood pressure.

It maintains and regulates our daily physiological activity cycles.

It has a direct influence on our electrolyte balance, day-night rhythm and also our feeling of hunger and thirst.

All the above activities and many more is directly dependent on the ability of hypothalamus to release, inhibit and instruct hormonal activities happening throughout our body in various endocrine glandular system.

It is just like an app (application) in your mobile phone by which you can control your purchases, and payments and also delete unwanted or unsolicited messages. In other words Hypothalamus is the leader in the endocrine glandular system a pictorial representation depicts this special gland and its effects on our ageing process.

The pituitary gland is a much smaller gland in size than hypothalamus and sits at the base of our brain just below the hypothalamus. Both these glands are very important to the functioning of the endocrine system and together they form the control centre for the entire neuroendocrine system and activate many vital activities.

Like the hypothalamus Pituitary gland also releases hormones which are very important for the activity of the other endocrine glands. Some of the hormones released by the pituitary are following which activate or stimulate other glands for our physiological functions;

- It stimulates our thyroid glands by releasing Thyroid Stimulating Hormones (TSH).
- Stimulates our Adrenal glands by releasing Adrenocorticotropic hormone (ACTH)
- Releases growth hormones GH) to maintain the growth of children in their developing years. It also helps adults to build up muscle mass and bone density.
- Releases Prolactin to stimulate the increased production of breast milk for young mothers and lactating women.
- Antidiuretic Hormone (ADH) regulates and balances water and sodium levels within our body.
- There are several other hormone systems that the Pituitary gland controls e.g. Follicle-stimulating hormone (FSH) and Luteinizing hormone (LH) which assists the normal functioning of the ovaries and testes.
- Oxytocin is a hormone that is essential for women during child birth. Its main function is to stimulate the contraction of the smooth muscle in the uterus to facilitate the birthing process.

The glands of the neuroendocrine system keep an eye over our glands and organs twenty-four-seven by sending messages via the chemical messengers our hormones. This is done specifically in the form of instruction to increase or reduce their activity and thus their functions.

Malfunctioning of the neuroendocrine system happens if the production and secretion of hormones are inadequate; either not enough or more than enough.

Under these circumstances following can be noticeable in the growth (gigantism and acromegaly), sugar metabolism (diabetes mellitus), excessive consumption of water and urination (diabetes insipidus), malfunction in reproductive organs and system (erectile dysfunction, menstrual disorders) etc.

Sometime normal growth in children can also be affected e.g. dwarfism and several other diseases.

The question is can we live without the glands of our endocrine system? The simplest answer is yes, depending on which endocrine gland we can live without.

However, adequate medication with missing hormones from the gland must be supplemented daily. Life will possibly be much restricted but nonetheless we will still continue to live on.

There are many chemicals both manmade and natural that we encounter on a daily basis that have a negative influence on the functioning of the endocrine glands. These chemicals which are often **called "endocrine system disrupters (ED)"** have adverse effects on humans and other animals to varying degrees. Some of these chemical disrupters we need to be careful of are......

Phthalates — used in making plastics and food wrappings and packaging, they are also used in certain cosmetics e.g. body lotions for skin adhesion properties, toys, and even in medical devices such as disposable gloves, blood bags catheters etc. It is quite a common ingredient to make the plastic more flexible.

Bisphenol-A (BPA) —finds use in the manufacture of polycarbonate plastics and epoxy resins. BPA is also used in plastic drinking bottles, the internal lining of some drink cans and food product storage containers.

Dioxins — dioxins are chemical contaminants which are produced when waste is incinerated, environmental burning, and also results from waste generated from several industrial processes. This gets into our food chain and causes contamination and accumulation in our body particularly the endocrine system here it causes the most damage.

Triclosan — it is added to many house hold products used to reduce or prevent bacterial contamination such as soaps, body washes, cosmetics, oral hygiene products etc.

It is added to some antibacterial soaps and body washes, toothpastes, and some cosmetics—products regulated by the U.S. Food and Drug Administration (FDA).

Pesticides, Herbicides and Fungicides (PHandF) — many common household (PHandF) are endocrine disrupters (ED). These can affect the functions of normal endocrine hormones by binding at the endocrine hormone receptor sites. Also, these ED interact with several neurotransmitter messaging systems and cause disruption to normal endocrine hormone functions. Several of these are very commonly used such as DDT (Dichlorodiphenyltrichloroethane is an insecticide), Chlorpyrifos (*it* is an organophosphate insecticide), Atrazine (is a chlorinated herbicide), 2, 4-D, Glyphosate (used very commonly in weed killers) and many more. Some of these are highly neuro-toxic.

Since COVID-19, everyday cleaning has become an essential part of our daily life and therefore we all have to some extent obsessed with cleaning products and implements which generally get stored under the sink or wash room selves. A common ingredient of these products is 2-butoxyethanol (EGBE) which is linked with animal reproductive problems.

(*Ref:wwwn.cdc.gov/TSP/PHS/PHS.aspx?phsid=345andtoxid=61*)

In the highly industrialized society that we now live in with convenience being the keyword, it is very likely that we have forgotten the art of taking help from mother nature, and her endless bounties to whip up concoctions that are just as effective if not more to reduce the effects of myriads of chemical and environmental pollution we subject ourselves to in our everyday life. Through just breathing often polluted air, drinking contaminated water in our drinking water system, food chain, household products (cleaning, personal care, oral-hygiene and others) we are risking our longevity and well-being.

Science has now proved in many instances that even low doses of endocrine-disrupting chemicals (ED) may be unsafe and injurious to our health.

So how can we help ourselves to keep our endocrine system healthy? The generalized answer is:

- Regular exercise, good nutrition and a good quality multi-vitamin supplement
- For senior citizens regular medical check-ups and follow-ups
- Follow medical and care advice when it comes to medical interventions
- Understand your family history of endocrine problems; most commonly issues such as diabetes, thyroid, Multiple Endocrine Neoplasia, Congenital adrenal hyperplasia, etc., and many more that I had not even heard of.

- Follow basic hygiene conditions, try to create indoor filtered air environment.
- Where possible avoid common (ED) containing chemicals in your day-to-day existence.

Common sense is the key to wellness and good health.

(Diagramme of our endocrine gland system)

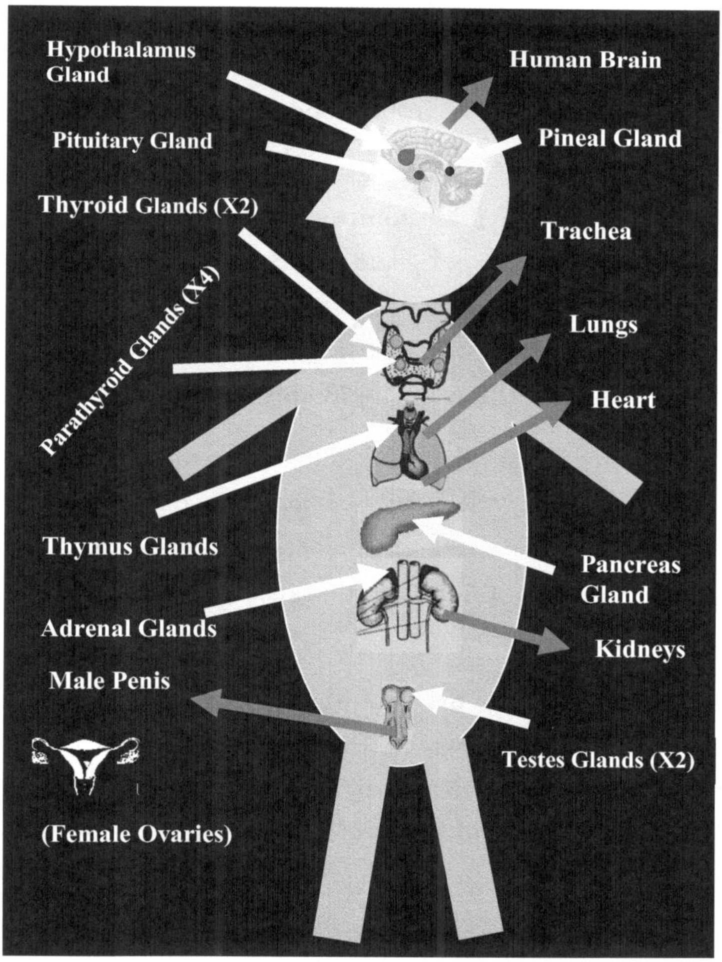

(In the diagramme the lighter arrows are pointing to the gland and the darker arrows are pointing to the relevant Organs).

Many of us have heard of the following terminology related to the removal of a particular endocrine gland from our body.

Pancreatectomy: In case of serious defects in our pancreas such as pancreatitis, cancer of the pancreas and other progressive degeneration requires the partial or complete removal of the pancreas gland. This can affect the metabolism of glucose and in general carbohydrate metabolism due to the unavailability of insulin and other pancreatic juices required in our digestive processes. But life still continues on normally with the required supplementation of insulin and the digestive enzymes that a perfectly working pancreas offers.

Thyroidectomy: Thyroidectomy is similar surgical procedure for removing part of our thyroid glands. The hormones produced by this endocrine gland control many of our important physiological activities and its removal, partial or otherwise makes us dependent on the required hormones particularly Thyroxine for as long as we live.

Pinealectomy is a surgical procedure that removes the pineal gland when a pineal tumour, which could be benign or malignant, is detected. The pineal gland is a part of the endocrine system that is responsible for creating melatonin, a hormone that plays a huge role in the body's circadian rhythm.

Hypophysectomy is the removal of our pituitary gland. Our pituitary gland is also known as The Master and originated from the combination of ancient Greek words "hupo' and phu'sis" meaning "Lying Under" for its position under the side of the brain. The name pituitary probably comes from Latin *pītuītārius*. It is a ductless endocrine gland which squirts the hormones directly into the blood stream. Its removal surgically due to a malfunction of the pituitary gland system, cancerous growth, benign and/or malignant tumours, etc. may cause the patient a lifelong requirement for administering the pituitary hormones.

Besides these more common removals of certain endocrine glands, there are others, such as, **Adrenalectomy,** is the surgical removal of one or both of the adrenal glands.

Parathyroidectomy, like the Thyroidectomy is the partial or entire removal of the entire parathyroid gland.

Total Pancreatectomy - This procedure removes the entire pancreas, and often the gallbladder, part of the stomach and small intestine, and the spleen as well. This is quite a major surgical procedure and takes place if absolutely necessary. Often a **Partial Pancreatectomy** is performed to rectify pancreatic gland insufficiencies due to tumours, benign growths and other issues for remedial action.

It must be note that removal of a particular endocrine gland entirely is subject to a careful medical consideration and future prognosis and care regime such that the survival of the patient is not at risk.

Looking at our organ impairments as we age it is also important to be aware of the systemic insufficiencies.

Having discussed the Endocrine Glands in our body let me touch upon a collection of another group of important glands called the **Exocrine Glands**. These glands are located all over the body and work in distinct ways to protect our body and help with various body functions. They excrete fluids that flow through ducts (tubes) into the body surface that helps various body functions; the diagramme provides their location and functions.

For example, the lacrimal glands also known as the tear glands which excretes a liquidly substance to keep our eyes moist from drying out. It keeps our eyes lubricated and protects against dry eyes syndrome.

Our sebaceous glands (also known as sweat glands) are located on the skin surface of the epithelial layer and release an oily substance called sebum into the hair follicles and skin pores to keep our skin and hair surface lubricated and protects from cracking due to dryness and also helps to keep the temperature of the body regulated. It also puts an additional barrier to protection against infection.

Salivary glands produce saliva a concoction of various enzymes and digestive chemicals which start the digestive process in the mouth; and so on.

Our Exocrine Glands

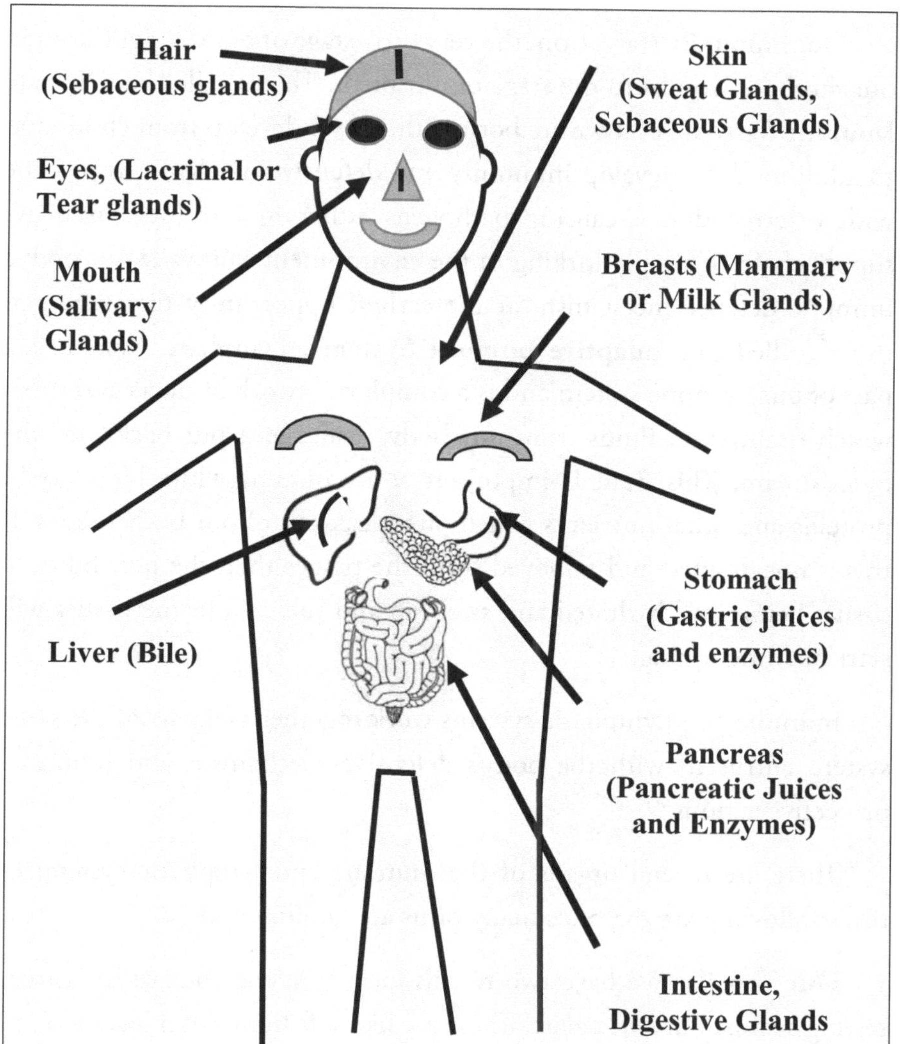

Immune and lymphatic system: Our immune system is an important functional system which keeps us protected from external contaminants such as pollution, pollens etc. and microbes or micro-organisms such as bacteria, viruses and fungal parasites.

Our immunity starts from the very early stage of our life right from in our mother's wombs to the stage of our birth. This is called the **"innate Immune System"** that we are born with. As we develop from childhood to adulthood we develop immunity and defensive mechanisms to cope with external disease-causing pathogens either in our food or drink supply chain or simply lurking in the environment to invade our body's immune defence mechanism at the earliest opportunity that they get; this is called the **"adaptive Immune System".** Lymphatic System is a part of our immune system and is a complex network of ducts and tubes which drain extra fluids from our body tissues and put back into the bloodstream. This fluid is important as it contains white blood cells, proteins and other nutrients which often leak out of our body tissues. If this is not drained and removed from the tissues then the possibility of tissues being over hydrated and swell up and the cells in the tissues will start malfunctioning.

Immune and Lymphatic systems work together as a part of the same system entrusted with the body's defensive mechanism and immune-protective actions.

There are several organs of the immune and lymphatic system; of these following are the once many of us are familiar with.

Our Tonsils: We have two tonsils located at the back of the throat resting against our soft palate. These are like soft lumps of masses around 2-2.5 centimetres in size. They mainly help prevent germs from entering our body through the mouth and the nasal passageway and contain white blood cells as a preventive measure to kill germs. Our tonsils are often known as vestigial organs which is left behind since our early evolutionary days since we do not have much use of them in our modern anatomical set up.

Cornélio Celsus, in the 1st century B.C., was the first to describe tonsillectomy surgery. He reported the procedure performance for dissection and removal of the structures (*Ref: Nogueira Junior JF, Dr. Americo RR, Stamm RG, Hirata CW. A brief history of Tonsillectomy. Int. Arch. Otorhinolaryngol 2006; 10(4): 314-317*).

Our spleen: It is an important organ but not absolutely necessary for our survival. It is a relatively small organ about the size of our fists. It is located in the vicinity of our liver on the left upper side of our abdomen or stomach. It stores and filters blood and helps in manufacturing white blood cells and antibodies which are important as it gives our immune system a fighting chance to ward off the invading infections.

Our spleen is important for our immune defence mechanism, we can survive without the spleen if need be as the liver can take over most functions of the spleen.

Lymph nodes: Lymph nodes or glands are tiny pea like structure (even smaller) which are located throughout our body (see the picture *Ref: Health Direct; https://www.healthdirect.gov.au/immune-system*). These nodules contain a concentration of white blood cells to fight infections. Due to their strategic location throughout our body including the neck, armpits, groin, around the gut, and between the lungs they form a very important part of the defence network and drain excess fluid from nearby organs and deposit into bloodstream thus keeping our tissues and cell integrity intact.

Thymus gland: Thymus glands have been referenced above, but additionally to being a part of the endocrine gland system it also holds a major role in the nurturing of the T-Lymphocyte cells (interesting to note T refers to Thymus) which is essential for the development of our adaptive immune system. Our body's white blood cells (also called lymphocytes) migrate from the bone marrow tissues where they are formed to our thymus glands and become specialised T-Cells to fight infections. So in other words our Thymus glands are like training grounds for the white blood cells to be combat ready.

Bone marrow: Bone marrow is essential for manufacturing our blood cells (both white cells and the red cells). It is the soft spongy tissue inside our bones. Red blood cells carry oxygen while the white blood cells fight infection. Our bone marrow also produces platelets (also called Thrombocytes). These are very small blood cell fragments which causes blood the clot and prevent excess bleeding.

There are other specialized cells called the B – Cells (B-Lymphocytes) a specialized white blood cells which are an essential part of our immune system that make antibodies. Whenever an antigen or a foreign particle or fragment enters our blood stream by way of food or drink supply chain or environmental contaminant then the B-cells spring into action by producing numerous antibodies by cloning themselves and neutralize those foreign antigens with the help of the T-cells.

As mentioned the B-cells are specialized white blood cells or lymphocytes; so why they are named B- cells. In simple terms B stands for Bone marrow where it is produced. But historically B comes from **"Bursa of fabricius, (BF)"** which was described by Fabricius ab Aquapendente in the 1600s. BF is a small fluid-filled sac which is located at the end of the gastro-intestinal tract (gut) in birds.

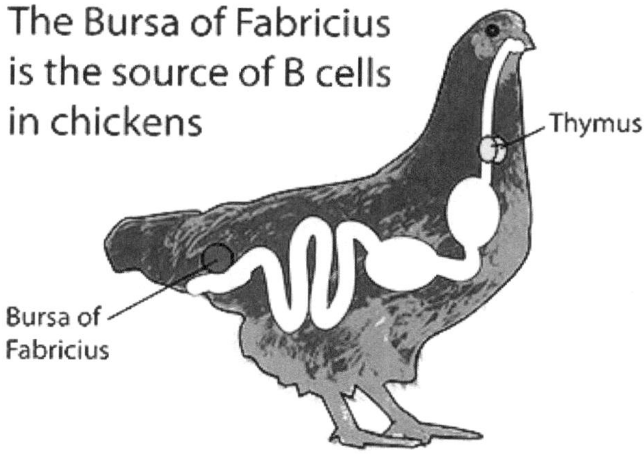

(Ref: https://www.fortislife.com/content/b-is-for-bursa)

In the 1950s and 60s, two researchers Bruce Glick and Timothy Chang from Ohio State University (USA) determined that the sac of Bursa was the only site of B-cell production to maturity in chicken. They also discovered that bursectomized chickens were incapable of producing B-cells to counteract the infectious effects of Salmonella. This opened up a whole new concept in immunology with respect to the T-cell (Thymus) and the B-cell (Sac of Bursa in birds). In mammals the B-cell originates in the bone marrow and hence called B-cells.

Peyer patches: Payer patches are funny conglomerate of fibrous tissues located in the **ileum area** which is the very end area of the small intestine. This is where the final leftover bits of the ingested food is processed and absorption of water and nutrients takes place. The payer patch is not to be confused with the **Intestinal Villi** located all-around of the intestinal lining projecting outwards in thin elongated structures. These structures (The Villi) allow an efficient absorption of nutrients from foods all around the intestine lining by increasing the available surface area for absorption.

Payer patches play an important role in monitoring and controlling the intestinal bacterial content and population and in doing so prevent an overload of bacterial growth in the intestine. Payer's patches also contain the B-cells, T-cells and a specialized cells called the M-cells (The Microfold Cells) which help destroy the antigens. Antigens as described earlier are foreign bodies such as viruses, fragments of bacteria, etc.

Adenoids: Most of us have experienced Ear infections and ear aches, inflamed sinuses, sleep apnoea etc. from time to time. All of these are most probably due to adenoid infection. There are two adenoid glands which sit between our nostrils at the back of the throat. These are flesh lymph tissues and like our tonsils help kill germs which invade our body through the nasal airways and the mouth. Sometimes in the process of defending our body they get inflamed and swollen resulting in certain common respiratory idleness as mentioned earlier.

Adenoid glands are mostly active during childhood to young adulthood and start shrinking in size around the age of 5-10 years of age and disappear at the time of teenage to young adulthood.

It is very rarely that adenoids pose a problem in adults and as we age adenoids also age with us and only an eminence (a raised structure) is left over as a patch of tissue.

Adenoids may also be classified as vestigial organs like the tonsils as they do not have much use in young adults to older population; but, as they serve an important immune defence in babies to young children it is still an important part of our immune/lymphatic system.

Lymphatic vessels: These are a network of tubes and ducts that are responsible for carrying out leaked fluid from the cells, tissues and tissue areas and carried back into the blood stream. There can also be plasma leaking out of fine capillary vessels into our muscles, tissues and various organs which then drains out into the lymphatic ducts and carried back to the blood stream. These fluids carry waste materials such as dead blood cells, debris from fragments of damaged cells, toxins and other pathogens resulting from our immune response to external viral or bacterial invasion and also unabsorbed nutrients. The Veins in our circulatory system carry this toxic fluid to our lungs, kidneys and liver for filtration and removal from the body by way of urine. The nutrients are recycled and reabsorbed by various tissues, the oxygen depleted blood is re-oxygenated into our lungs and this cycle is repeated over and over again. Just a bit of trivia of interest; our kidneys weighing around 160g each filters almost 200 litres of blood in a 24-hour period and if we say that we have around 4 litres of blood in an adult body then our entire blood is filtered at least 50 times in a 24-hour period. Amazing feat of performance by such a tiny organ.

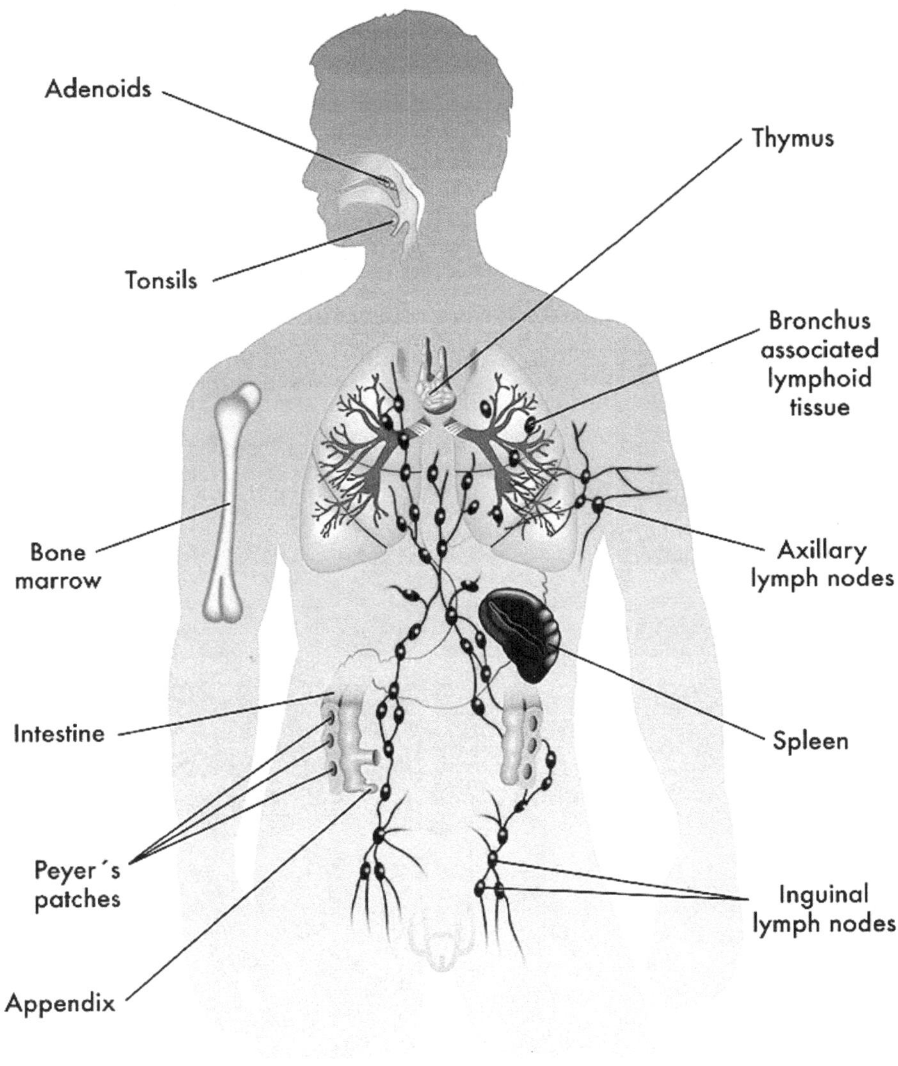

Organs of our immune system (Ref: Health Direct https://www.healthdirect.gov.au/immune-system)

Integumentary system: This is our body's outermost covering or simply "Our Skin". It protects our body from external elements such as heat, shock, environmental factors and infections which can easily penetrate into our body through open wounds. So, our skin is the first line of defence as it protects our internal organs and keeps them safe from external elements. The structure of our skin is relatively simple and consists of an external layer of hair, several glands which are strategically placed in the epidermis (outermost layer of the skin), the dermis (which is the middle layer of the skin) and the subcutaneous layer which is the deepest layer of our skin. Each layer has its own designated tasks to perform.

Glands which are located in various layers of our skin collectively called exocrine glands as mentioned earlier opposed to the endocrine glands which are not connected to any ducts or channels rather endocrine glands open directly into the blood stream for the hormones these glands produce can be directly carried by blood to the receptor sites where they are needed.

Exocrine glands located in our integumentary system on the other hand are connected to ducts to carry the secreted products mostly into the epithelial cells which cover the internal and external surface covering of our body as described earlier in this chapter.

A simplified diagramme of various layers of our skin:

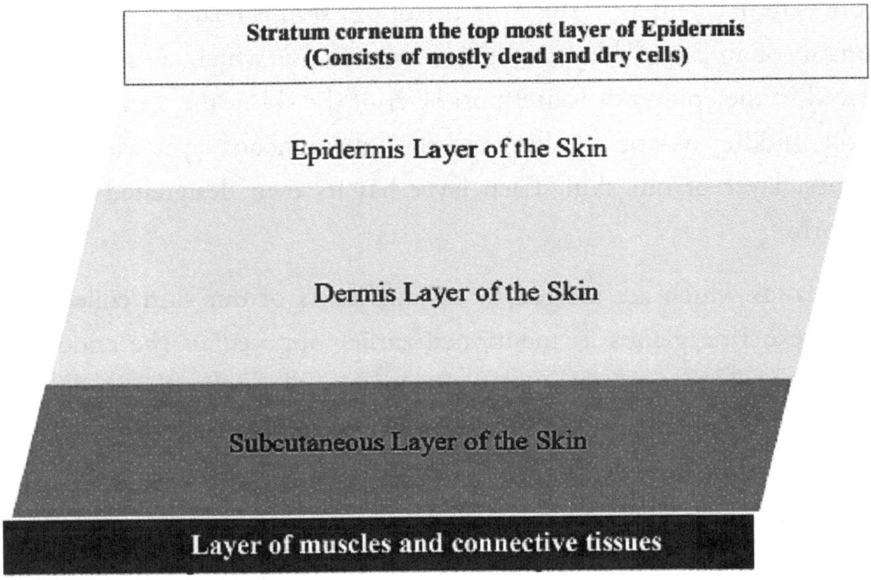

As we age our skin undergoes massive changes and leads to venerability of skin diseases ranging from mild to severe. The production of new hair follicles, and skin lubricants, e.g., sweat, oils and fatty secretions are diminished due to reducing numbers of ducts and capillary blood vessels under the epidermis and the dermis layers of the skin making the outer layer of the skin more prone to micro-bleeding and easy to bruise.

With all the above causes' **Appearance** is the earliest sign of ageing skin with exceptions of external makeover and sensible use of skin tonics.

Under normal circumstances in elderly skin, the following most common changes are likely to happen;

Dryness of the skin leads to cracking and minor splits. These create minor pores and channels which allow infections and foreign particles (from environmental pollution to get inside the inner layers of the skin.

The sebaceous and the sweat glands lack in their ability to produce lubricants thus unable to keep the skin moist and provide a protective barrier of oily layer. It also loses its ability to maintain the wetness and temperature resulting in dry and itchy skin.

Sagging of the skin is caused by loss of collagen and elastin which are proteins which are responsible for the firmness, elasticity and suppleness of our skin. As we age our body slows down in its ability to bio-synthesise both proteins in the required quantities as a result the ageing skin sags. Another reason being as we age we lose our weight and the excess skin from lost weight tends to sag. Most noticeably sagging tends to be more prominent along the eye area, chin neck and throat, the forearm area, stomach, waist area etc.

Photo-ageing and skin **pigmentation** can also happen at old age. Due to thinning of the skin 7-dehydrocholesterol is not available to protect the skin from Sun's rays by converting into vitamin D causing some damage to the skin. Also, the sun-burns can cause the skin to darken and tan much quicker than a younger healthy skin. Some of these sun burn spots can become cancerous and lead to more serious skin diseases. Thinner skin also can cause blistering and skin lesions.

Shedding of our unwanted dead skin cells: As we age cells from skin's outermost layer, the topmost layer of the epidermis die off and begin to shed. The rate of shedding depends on dryness, loss of oils and lubrication, lack of cleanliness and other factors. It has been reported that around 40,000 dead cells can shed from the epidermis layer in an hour which equates to around a million cells a day and an astounding 350 million cells in a year. Although I found this value to vary greatly in several sources, I have chosen to report this reference (*https://www.skincancercentres.com.au/blog/what-causes-dead-skin-cell-build-up-and-how-can-you-treat-it-1*) (Reported July 2021, National skin cancer centres Australia) as a guide only.

It is important to exfoliate and cleanse our skin at all ages to facilitate the growth of new skin. Sometimes in older skin, the shedding does not take place consistently resulting in a build-up of dead skin causing skin lesions which if not treated appropriately can lead to serious skin diseases.

Osteopenia and osteoporosis: Although, loss in bone density and bone mass can start at any age in our infancy to adulthood due to genetic mutation in the CASR gene (Calcium-sensing receptor) which affects the normal functioning of parathyroid glands. As we age, there is a normal decline in calcium absorption from food and supplementation due to a weakness in our anatomical function, e.g., our intestine. Due to ageing the walls of the intestine grow thicker with the depletion of the calcium-absorbing receptors. Also, our kidneys due to impairments lose their functions; one of which is the reabsorption of calcium along the renal tubules.

One of the main reasons for the lack of calcium in the elderly population is the lack of calcium-enriched food intake and improper calcium supplementation and importantly low or no Vitamin D intake which assists in efficient calcium absorption.

Hypocalcemia (low calcium) causes Osteopenia and Osteoporosis which are the primary reasons for bone density and bone mass loss. Osteopenia is the first stage of Osteoporosis and both conditions if left untreated can cause serious damage to bone brittleness. Osteoporosis is one of the current and most talked about conditions in the elderly. Prevention is better than cure and it is up to us to have regular bone density scans regularly over the age of 65 and or as per your medical advice.

Bone shrinkage is also an issue for consideration and care in old age. However, it has been researched that bone shrinkage starts in our mid-adulthood. There are several reasons for bone shrinkage apart from the genetic or inherited causes. Our bones or the skeletal structure have the most distribution of calcium in our body. It is estimated that an adult body has a total Calcium around 1.3kg of this approx. 99% is used up in our skeletal structure. As we age it is estimated that over time our bones shrink about 1 inch (2.54cm). More in cases of Osteopenia, osteoporosis and other bone density issues. It has been suggested that between the ages of 30 and 70 we could lose 1inch and furthermore, from age 80 we start to lose more in height due to bone shrinkage. This causes a significant change in our gait and upright stance as we start to stoop. Shrinkage among the elderly population can also be caused by a decline in the joint fluid and the cartilage that supports bone structure e.g. our spinal column which also becomes shorter and we lose inches in height.

Sarcopenia is also related to the loss of bone density in older people and is just as important in elderly people's health care as Osteopenia and Osteoporosis are. All three diseases are related to bone density and mass and are equally critical to our health and well-being and therefore a priority in every elderly citizen's health care assessment programmes.

Sarcopenia has been discussed in some detail in the next chapter.

Loss in balance and stability:

It is not un-usual that as we age we tend to lose our balance and steadiness. This can severely impede our movements, sense of independence and confidence. Trips and falls can be noticeable, and our movements can be seriously restricted. There are several physiological and psychological issues that can cause a loss of balance and steadiness as we grow old. But simply let us consider the most common causes and look at a few remedial actions.

First, our balance is related to our strength and muscle flexibility, both of which diminish with age. Loss of bone density and mass and the flexibility and tensile strength of our lower core muscles cause a serious loss of the ability in our lower torso to support our weight and structure. This not only causes back pain but also loss in our movement and balance. The other aspect of this is the inability of our heart to pump blood as efficiently as in our younger days causing a lowering of our blood pressure which also causes a temporary loss of balance when we make some sudden moves such as standing up from a sitting position and walking from a standstill position, etc. Under such circumstances, we may lose our balance for a short time only but recover when the blood pressure gets back to our normal range. This is an individual thing and varies from situation to situation. However, point to remember is that this momentary lapse in our balance can be enough to tip us over causing a trip or a fall.

Why did I mention psychological issues in the context of loss of balance? Simple, as we age we have a number of thoughts going through our heads as to how we can protect ourselves; and as falls are a common denominator for hospitalization or home care situations we as oldies are thinking of this and maybe our independent living and get over-protective a reason enough to succumb to a loss of balance.

With a good diet, supplementing with appropriate nutrients and regular exercises can enhance our bone density and mass and also improve the strength, flexibility and suppleness of our inner core muscles which are attached to our lower back and spine. This may provide additional firmness for the inner core muscles and the lower bones from hip to the Femur and associated bone structures, e.g., Tibia and Fibula to strengthen and hold every thin in place to give us the additional balance and steadiness that we so need in our old age.

There is another issue I want to touch upon is the **sensory information** across the brain and our sensory organs which has some bearing on our balance, e.g., the brain signals our relevant muscles or sensory organs to perform required activities, in this case to steady our balances, etc., or our visions to warn about uneven surface which may trigger a trip or a fall. As we age, our neurons (these are messenger cells that carry to-and-fro messages from the brain to sensory organs and back via the nervous system; peripheral and central nervous systems).

Weaker neural system with ageing causes our neurons to become less effective in carrying out the orders from the brain due to many neurons dying. As the neural system is responsible for all the activities we perform as a living entity e.g. movements, sensory perceptions (seeing, touching, tasting, hearing and smelling), our basal functions (these are our biological functions happening internally within our body e.g. breathing, cellular metabolisms, digestive processes, our circulation, cell necrosis and cell production, etc.), it is very important for a healthy living that our neural system is active and functional to prevent many old age impairments.

Trips and falls in old age can be very debilitating as it can severely restrict their daily activities and often leave them inactive for extended period of time eventually causing death.

Let's leave this morbid subject behind and get on to a livelier topic of diet and lifestyle consideration for our elderly population (me included) in the next chapter.

Chapter 5

DIETARY, SUPPLEMENTARY AND LIFESTYLE CONSIDERATIONS FOR ELDERLY CITIZENS

"In old age, harmony of body, mind, and soul becomes essential. The keys: good nutrition, balanced diet, and healthy living."

– Jay Das ... 2024

As we age, we not only face psychological, physiological and environmental challenges but importantly nutritional challenges also in order to keep up with the daily nutritional demands.

There are mainly two considerations at play here in the management of a senior's nutritional status; one the issue of mal-nutrition or under-nutrition and the second availability of adequate nutrition.

Physiological and psychological changes in older people are important considerations along with their socio-economic status. Changes in the physical and mental status bring certain implications that if not addressed and recognised by seniors can lead to nutritional deficiencies.

Physiological changes, as we age can develop due to a low requirement in the food intake, but nonetheless the nutritional requirement remains pretty much the same or more depending on the physical activity levels. But the point to make here is that everyone young or old has a basic energy need to keep their most common physiological functions active. This basic energy requirement to perform simple biological tasks such as breathing, walking, lying down, or even doing nothing consumes energy. Apart from this our body will require additional calories to maintain and perform internal functions to keep us alive.

This energy in fact comes from the intake of food which will input a certain amount of calories into the system. But in order to maintain numerous biochemical functions happening within the body requires specific nutrients which the food taken in must provide.

Young or old we all require a basic amount of energy to keep our bodily functions alive. This basic energy requirement is known as the Basal Energy Requirement which is the minimum amount of energy we need to keep our bio-functions going, it does not matter if we are sleeping or awake; doing hard and strenuous work or just relaxing and doing nothing;

energy is still expended. So, before anything else, we must acquire this energy which can only come from food intake which gets converted into energy deep within our cellular structure in the mitochondria. Once we have made allowance for this energy to be available for our bodily functions, we need to intake more food to produce more energy for doing daily chores, e.g., walking, breathing, running, talking and many other physical activities that come naturally to us as human beings. In general, we divide our composite energy into two categories; obviously, these two main categories can then be subdivided into several other sub-categories.

Let me explain what energy is. Fundamentally energy is the power that drives us and allows us to carry out all the daily activities around us that we do to survive. Every basic movements we conduct expends energy and if we lack in energy then those movements cannot be done and we become impaired in some form or other which affects the quality of our life.

Modern Science categorizes energy into several categories; movement energy, heat energy, electrical energy, chemical energy, potential energy, kinetic energy mechanical energy, etc., just to name a few. Some of these energies are human creations, e.g., bombs which pack in unlimited energy for destruction; nuclear energies are classic examples. Then we have energy that we harvest from nature for our benefit for example, hydro-electric energy, solar energy and wind powered energies which we use in our daily lives. Then there is another kind of energy that is very personal to us; energy which we store and utilize within our body to sustain our lives. We produce this energy within our body fuelled by the foods and drinks we consume. The energy produced within our body is highly dependent on the quality of fuel we are providing our body. Just like a computer, the quality of data output is dependent on the quality of data input. It is as good as the person driving it. Similarly, our body is as good as we conduct it. If we maintain our body with regular exercise and our quality of food and supplement intake is of good quality then, the chances are that our body will thrive and our quality of life will be that much better.

Now let us see how we can categorise our body's energy requirement and utilization.

The first consideration is the basic energy that our body needs to conduct the primary body functions. We do not see these functions being carried out but they are being performed within our body 24 hours a day 7 days a week non-stop. These functions are conversion of food intake into fundamental energy molecules (e.g., ATP molecule Adenosine Triphosphate which is also known as the energy currency).

Transportation activities; this is a network of transport service to various parts of our body; for example, transporting blood and nutrients into various tissues and cells. Transport network is quite complex as the system not only transports nutrients but also various chemicals and biochemical, e.g., enzymes, hormones, oxygen, neurons, neurotransmitters and myriads of specialized compounds and components required for our cells and tissues to function and live-on. Then there is homeostasis a self-regulating process which keeps the body's internal condition consistent, maintenance of temperature and blood pressure within a consistent range, functions of organs for example keep our digestive systems going.

This energy that our body needs to keep our vital internal processes running is called the Basal Metabolic Rate (BMR) and is a quite significant chunk of the energy that our body produces from our food intake. It can be as high as 70% of our body's total energy expenditure which is dependent on our age, gender body structure, BMI, etc.

The next largest requirement is movement energy that is required for our various daily chores. These include walking, running, doing housework, working at a workplace, schooling, sports and exercise and many more external activities that are required to be undertaken in the process of our living.

Then there is another category which perhaps expends the least amount of energy during individual activity, e.g., sleeping, sitting and doing nothing. This is called sedentary or energy expended at rest.

Below is a table of generalising data for some of the popular activities and energy expended. I found the data presented by

Harvard Health www.health.harvard.edu "diet-and-weight-loss (Calories burned in 30 minutes of leisure and routine ...) is quite handy and a good useful reference.

Calories burned in 30 minutes:

Activities	125lbs/57kg person	155lbs/70kg Person	185lbs/84kg Person
Cooking	57	70	84
Sleeping	19	22	26
Reading: sitting	34	40	47
Standing in line	28	35	41
Slow Dancing	90	108	125
Fast Dancing	180	216	252
Shopping (with cart)	85	106	126
Gardening: general	135	162	189
Mowing Lawn(Push, Power)	135	162	189
Stretching (Hatha Yoga)	120	144	168
Bicycling 12-15.9 miles/hour	300	360	420

Swimming (General)	180	216	252
Walking (4 miles/ hour)	135	175	189
Tai Chi (exercises)	120	144	168
Running (7.5miles/ hour)	375	450	525
Running (cross country)	255	316	377
Tennis: general	210	252	294
Golf: (carrying clubs)/using cart	165/105	198/126	231/147
Weight lifting (General)	90	108	126
Boxing (sparring)	270	324	378
Soccer: general	210	252	294

The more intense the activity the more calories are burned. For example, in a person weighing 70kg following comparisons can be made. Walking at a slower pace at 3.5 mph will burn 133 calories but walking at a slightly brisk pace at 4 mph will burn 175 calories a difference of around 42 Calories. Running at 5mph will burn 288 calories, but running at 10mph will burn more than double the calories. Similarly, low impact aerobics will burn off 198 calories as compared with high impact aerobics which will burn off for you 252 calories, around 254 calories more. Physical activity is important for all ages, young adulthood to advance aged seniors. It is so important especially that all senior above 60 years old in our society must do some form of physical workout to stay healthy. For seniors, brisk walking 30 minutes a day could be the difference between living a normal ageing life and a healthy life. Normal life for most seniors of advancing ages is fraught with mild to severe health issues. Physical activities (depending on age and physical capabilities), mild weight training and other socially involved activities such as swimming, a game of golf, tennis, dancing and other outdoor activities, e.g., yoga, tai chi, bicycling, etc. have been proven methods for a healthy life. I don't mean that, only physical activity is the way to good health and longevity, but a full assessment of the holistic lifestyle itself is necessary. Just a few minutes a day of involved physical activity may help with the following irregularities in our lifestyle; It may assist with your sleep patterns. A good night's rest may bring some relief in blood pressure normalization.

Temporary relief in joint aches and pains.

Much required relief from anxiety, stressful conditions, symptoms of depression and general feel-good feelings are all positive flow-on from a good night's restful sleep.

For further reference on this subject check out the reports from the Centre for Disease Control and Prevention (CDC) the US-based health monitoring and advisory body.

(*www.cdc.gov/healthyweight/physical_activity/index.html) and (www.cdc.gov/physicalactivity/basics/pa-health/physical-activity-and-cancer.html*).

Both references are full of important information which are useful to the elderly population.

As the diagramme explains there is a 4 Point Strategy to Ageing Gracefully. Those who can bring all those strategic points together have better prospects in their ageing life.

Healthy Lifestyle and Old Age:

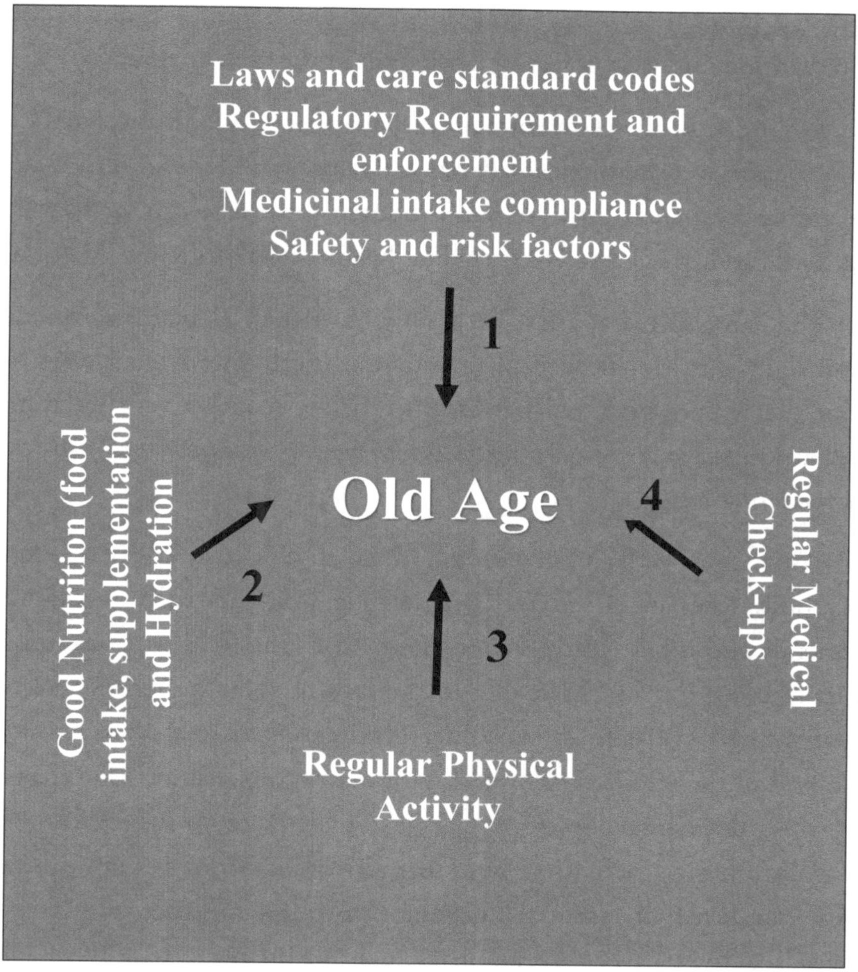

In an article 'Eating well' published by the Australian Government's *Eat for Health* initiative, it is noted that Australians should choose nutritious foods and drinks to protect health and reduce chronic disease risk."

In the above diagramme out of 4 strategic points, 3 are within the control of our lifestyle practices or with some external intervention. Strategy point 1 is a bit more involved and requires multi-factorial intervention and is a subject of discussion in the next chapter.

On the Australian Government Department of Health and Aged Care information website there are some very valuable and useful information regarding food and nutrition, and I thought those who can access it may get some additional awareness of their health and well-being.

You can also make use of an online Nutrient Calculator to estimate your daily nutritional need to maintain a healthy lifestyle at least from your dietary perspective. The reference below makes a very interesting and informative read. (*Ref: www.health.gov.au/topics/food-and-nutrition/about/eating-well*)

As we age, our lean body mass and metabolic rate decrease as a result our body loses its effectivity in absorbing nutrients such as vitamins, minerals and other essential ingredients from the food we consume on a daily basis. Furthermore, due to the lack of the required quantity of quality food available to the older [population in our society calorie intake and the required calories do not match and malnutrition may set in. This calorie intake in many cases is not adequate for the performance of daily physical activities. Malnutrition or inadequate calorie intake with low levels of essential nutrient absorption together with lack of physical activity causes several physiological ailments e.g. cardiovascular, skeletomuscular, respiratory and others in the elderly population causing disruption in their normal routine.

As I have mentioned above good nutrition and an active lifestyle are important for longevity and quality of life for the older population; the question is how to make it happen?

Malnutrition if not treated and managed in the elderly population can be fatal.

Apart from enriched protein portions in their regular diet, daily intake of nutritional supplement may become essential.

Let us address the issue of malnutrition in seniors.

Relevant questions to ask are, how does it happen, when does it happen and what are the solutions? There are several factors associated with this issue: infrequent and inadequate food intake. The quality of food taken may not be as nutritious as required. Elderly seniors who are living alone, due to their forgetfulness and inability to prepare fresh food for consumption are prime targets for malnutrition. Their socio-economic status also contributes to the cause. It is very likely that due to lack of available funds and prioritizing the need for the bare essentials, older seniors resort to substandard cheaper quality pre-packaged food items. This is quite common and prevalent in less affluent societies in almost every country rich or poor. Once the food is purchased with limited choices several psychological issues need also be considered, e.g., changes in sensory perceptions of the seniors (taste, appearance, smell and perhaps feel) may result in a low appetite and hence affect the over-all food intake.

If the food when displayed out of the packaging for preparation (heating, boiling or other complex cooking process, e.g., frying) does not psychologically appeal to the consumer it may put them off consuming it which leads to the proverbial "there goes the wasted meal" and increases the chances of malnutrition.

Assessing and addressing mal-nutrition in elderly people living alone or in a communal living situation is not often very easy. Each elderly may have certain requirements which needs to be addressed and programmed and monitored.

Assessment and care plans should be routinely monitored for elderly patients under professional care, and for those living alone in local governmental care facilities should be available on a periodic basis.

The four sensory perceptions although are anatomically based they have a profound influence on psychological factors as well. For example, if a senior citizen does not like the look of a meal or a particular item on the plate that can put him/her off. The same goes with the feel; a fruit may be too much or too little ripe giving the impression that the fruit may have gone off or still raw; an egg may be too hard or too soft. Not all elderly people have the same sensory perception and view each presentation differently in favour or against.

It is highly likely that a meal or a particular item served on a plate can put off a person young or old alike. This is just judging by the sight perception only and could have other negative consequences. But none the less these parameters in varying degrees have a strong bearing on food habits and intake.

Other anatomical issues caused by certain impairments such as health issues which may limit movements for sourcing foods, socio-economic limitations causing procurement issues are likely to cause disruption to their purchasing ability of quality foods. Other issues are lack of proper facilities (storage, food preparation) all contribute to poor food intake and may push them over the threshold of malnutrition.

Sometimes loneliness, depression, and anxiety can contribute to their declining urge to prepare meals and eat; this could result in diminished nutritional status.

Due to lack of exercise free hand and or with equipment, light weight training and exercises and others e.g. swimming, walking, mild sports (game of golf) the elderly population in our society start losing muscle mass. This could lead to a condition called Sarcopenia (also discussed in Ch. 2) causing loss of body muscle mass and strength. There is no definitive cure to this condition as it is not properly treatable using medication. However, using structured physical activity and weight training to improve strength and physical performance can assist in the recovery of,

and physical performance can assist in the recovery of muscle mass. A diet enriched in protein definitely adds to the recovery process. Apart from enriched protein portions in their regular diet, daily intake of nutritional supplements may become essential.

Malnutrition Causes and Management:

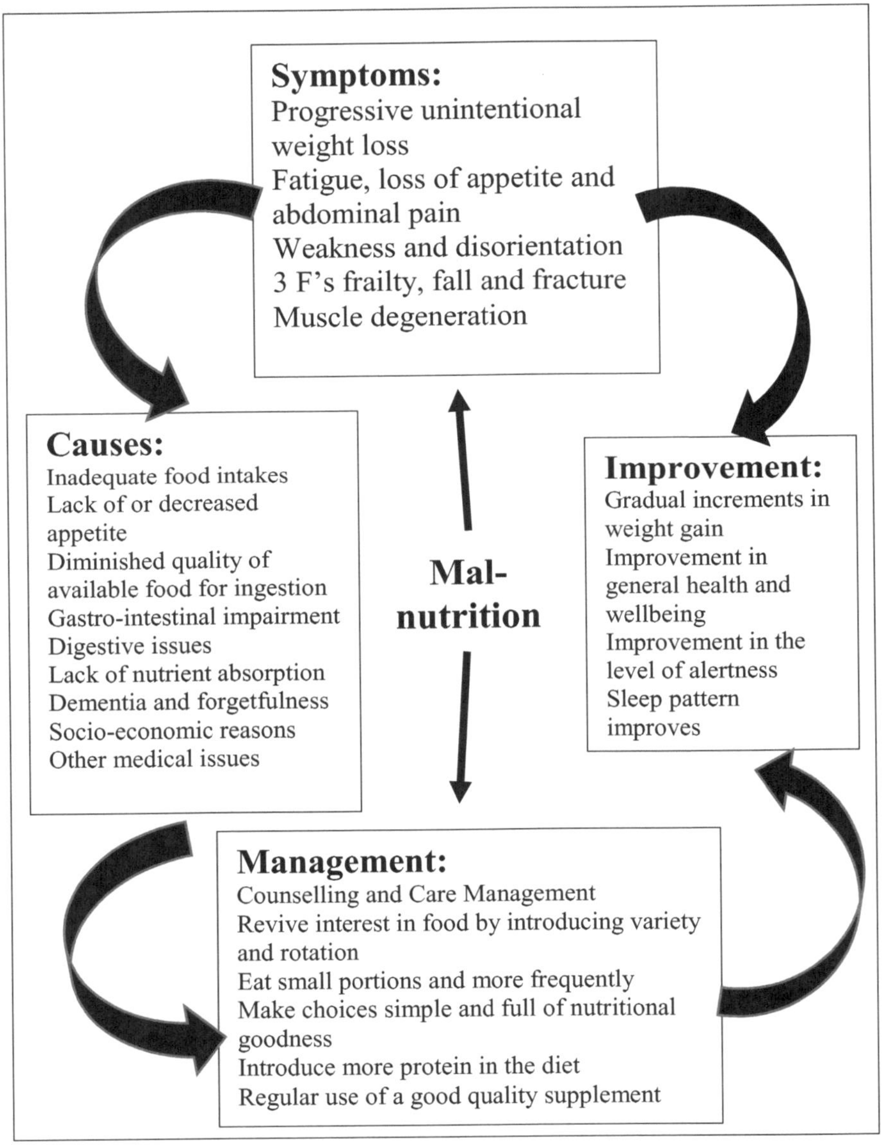

Virtually most of the diseases or health issues experienced by the elderly population can be traced back to their dietary and nutritional insufficiencies. E.g., Osteoporosis is predominantly related to a lack of calcium and vitamin D. Simply by increasing dairy products milk, cheese, yoghurt etc. and several soy products like tofu along with a bit of sunshine and/or vitamin D supplements could assist. However, it is important to maintain a regime of exercise, lightweight training and regular brisk walks and reduce the quantity of alcohol, smoking and drug abuse. We all should keep within our limits of endurance when practicing physical activities. Never overdo assuming more is good for health. Overdoing can do more harm than good. At the first sign of discomfort consult your health care practitioner and or a general practitioner.

Malnutrition can also cause weakness, dizziness, falls and fractures and often requires significant institutional care. Loss of immunity is also a significant factor associated with malnutrition.

The development of Sarcopenia

is quite prevalent in our older population. The degree of severity varies with age and a lack of physical activity and under-nourishment. It is characterized by progressive decline in the skeletal muscle mass and strength causing a severe restriction in the movement of the sufferers. These patients often require institutional care with particular attention to their physical activity and dietary needs.

The disease Sarcopenia in the elderly if not diagnosed in the early stages can be debilitating with a poor quality of life.

Inter-relationship between old age and Sarcopenia can be quite involved. It is suggested that Sarcopenia can affect at the age of 40 and rapidly decline in health condition by the age of 80 and 80 plus years when it is estimated that a loss of about 50% of muscle mass and strength can be lost. It is also a progressive degenerative muscle-wasting disease.

As a Sarcopenia patient advances in age, other associated old age-related diseases such as osteoporosis, diabetes, respiratory issues, and mental health issues can become of major significance; depending on the severity hospitalization is the only option for patient care. The other ill health aspect to watch out for is the three F's frailty, falls and fractures.

A simple diagrammatic representation can highlight the disease itself and its consequences for the sufferers.

(Further reading reference: *www.my.clevelandclinic.org/health/diseases/23167-sarcopinia*)

Sarcopenia and Challenges in Elderly Citizens

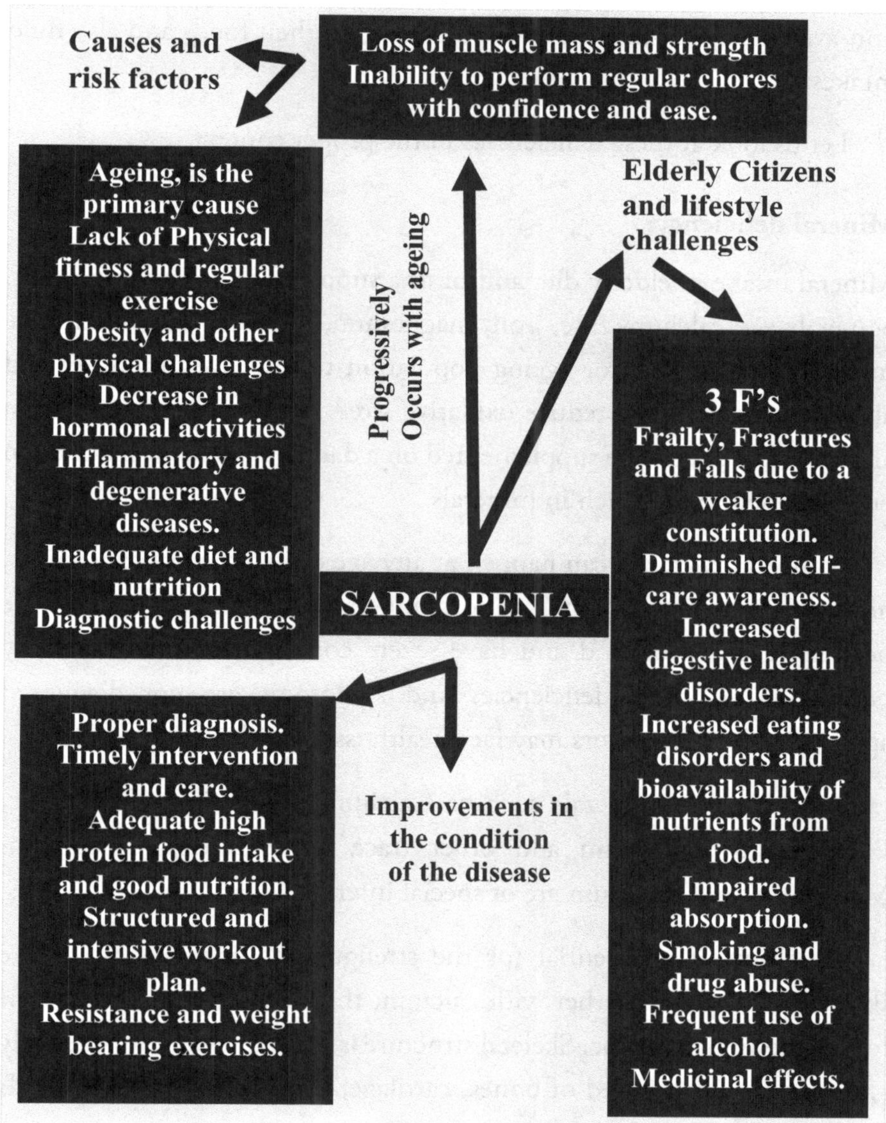

Loss of function, disability, and frailty:

Common nutritional deficiencies in the elderly are lack of protein intake, non-availability of vitamins and minerals from their foods and also fluid intakes.

Let us look at these deficiencies in the proper context.

Mineral deficiency:

Mineral intake in elderly diet and/or as a supplement is very important. Minerals e.g. calcium, zinc, iron, magnesium, selenium and other trace minerals are essential for ageing population to improve immunity and antioxidant activity to reduce oxidative stress in the elderly population and therefore should be supplemented on a daily basis and/or required to be consumed in food rich in minerals.

Mineral deficiency can happen at any age due to dietary constraints, however, in the elderly population mineral deficiencies can be more noticeable and profound and have severe consequences in the elderly population. If these deficiencies and symptoms are not diagnosed appropriately then seniors may face health issues with slow recovery.

Several macro-minerals such as Calcium, Magnesium, Iron, Zinc, Phosphorous, Potassium and other trace minerals e.g. Chromium, Manganese, and Selenium are of special interest.

Calcium: It is essential for the strength and fortification of the skeletal structure. Together with calcium, there is a strong requirement for magnesium and Zinc. Skeletal structure is the framework for the body and primarily composed of bones, cartilage, ligaments etc. which holds the body in an upright position.

Elderly people with age lose their bone density and strength as a result there is considerable weakness resulting in osteoporosis and Sarcopenia.

Calcium is essential for bone tissue and helps repair wear and tear of our skeletal structure. Our bone structure helps protect our internal organs from serious damage so, it is critical to maintain it at all ages. More so, in our elderly population.

Milk and dairy products (cheese, yoghurt) and fish with soft chewable bones (salmon, sardines) are the best sources and must be included in senior's diets. Many fortified foods including cereals, and fortified beverages (soy milk and other soy products) are also rich in calcium.

Almost all of the available calcium in our body is taken up by the bone and teeth structures the remaining available calcium which is less than about 2% finds its way into muscle, tissues and blood. Several other minerals e.g. Sodium interfere with calcium availability and therefore must be regulated.

It is important to note that more than 65% of adult Australians aged 50 years and over have osteoporosis or osteopenia due to significant or marginal calcium deficiency;

(*Ref: Healthy Bones Australia https://healthybonesaustralia.org.au " 2022/09*)

The Estimated Average Requirement (EAR) of calcium in a population over the age of 70 years and over is 1300mg daily.

A healthy calcium rich diet, additional calcium supplementation and a good quality vitamin D supplement together with meaningful exercise should go a long way for a healthy bone structure and general health and wellbeing.

Magnesium: Magnesium (Mg) deficiency in old age can be due to dietary insufficiencies and lack of absorption from the intestine. It is estimated that body's half the available Mg is in the bone structure and the rest available to most muscle and soft tissues and a significant portion is concentrated in the extracellular fluid which is the fluid outside the cellular structure.

Low magnesium concentration causes sleep and cognitive disorders ranging from mild to serious complications. Reports linking Mg deficiency to several disease states e.g. cardiovascular diseases, hypertension and stroke, cardio-metabolic syndrome and type 2 diabetes mellitus, airways constrictive syndromes and asthma, depression, stress-related conditions and psychiatric disorders, Alzheimer's disease (AD) and other dementia syndromes (*Ref: Nutrients. 2021 Feb; 13(2): 463.*). Muscular diseases such as muscle pain, chronic fatigue, and fibromyalgia have also been reported (ref. as above).

A diet consisting of fresh fruits, green vegetables, pulses and lentils, nuts and cereals are all good sources of magnesium.

The EAR for magnesium is 320mg daily.

Zinc: This important element is universally necessary for young adults to older populations globally. It has been estimated that up to 3 million serious infections occur yearly in Nursing homes in America (*https://www.mcknights.com/marketplace/the-importance-of-zinc-especially-for-the-elderly/ Joy Stephenson-Law March 2018*).

Infections in elderly population more commonly include diarrhoea caused by bacterial and/or parasitic infections, urinary tract infection (UTI), and resistance to common institutional bacterial infections such as Staphylococcus aureus (golden staph) and other germs, Pneumonia influenza, etc.

Among the elderly population who already have a lower threshold of antibiotic resistance and a declining immune system, it is not unusual that infectious diseases are the most common cause of their death.

It has been estimated that a third of the older population in America dies of infectious diseases, among these about 90% of the deaths occur due to pneumonia in the age group of 65 years and above

(*Am Fam Physician. 2001; 63(2):257-269 Mortality resulting from influenza also occurs primarily in the elderly*).

There are numerous publications reporting the benefits of taking zinc supplements to reduce the rate of infection in elderly people e.g. (*Ref: The American Journal of Clinical Nutrition, Vol 103, issue 3, 9. 941-951 March 2016 and https://lpi.oregonstate.edu/mic/minerals/zinc*)

Trace mineral deficiency including zinc in old people is quite common due to their impaired digestive and absorption function and therefore it is a good practice to top up their pool of zinc and other trace mineral by intake of trace minerals including zinc rich foods and also taking once a day zinc supplement.

Some of the food items which are good sources of zinc and many other essential minerals are:

Poultry (chicken and eggs)

Oysters

Nuts and seeds (e.g., chia seeds)

Grains e.g. oats

Green vegetables (spinach, beans, broccoli)

So, these foods are good to be added to the daily dietary intake in old age diet. Especially nuts which are also a rich source of selenium a trace mineral which is essential to our general health and wellbeing.

Zinc is a relatively safe mineral to take. It has been reported that over-intake of zinc either as a supplement or in the diet can be detrimental to health as it can cause nausea and vomiting, stomach upset, appetite loss, dizziness and headaches and also possible interaction with certain drugs e.g. antibiotics, Thiazide diuretics and rheumatoid arthritis drug penicil amine (*Cuprimine, Depen; Ref: https://www.mayoclinic.org/drugs-supplements-zinc/art-20366112*). It is also known and reported that too much zinc can interfere with iron and copper absorptions and levels as high as 142 mg daily can cause disruption to magnesium absorption and balance in the body; Zinc deficiency in older adults can cause delays in wound healing and changes in cognitive and psychological function (*Ref: https://ods.od.nih.gov/factsheets/Zinc-HealthProfessional/#en98*).

Zinc deficiency in older adults can cause delays in wound healing and changes in cognitive and psychological function

The EAR for zinc in the elderly population above 70 years is around 6.5mg daily. The RDI is 8 mg for women and 11 mg for men.

Zinc supplementation in the elderly population can be a positive step towards reducing the global burden of mild infections and hospitalization of elderly people suffering from mild to severe zinc deficiency related diseases.

Iron: Due to impaired digestive and absorption issues in the elderly, and lack of regular vitamin C intake, iron deficiency in the elderly population is not uncommon. Iron deficient anaemia in patients in aged and institutionalized care is quite prevalent, the common symptoms are fatigue and loss of energy, weakened immunity, lack of concentration and memory and forgetfulness. Iron deficient older age people often feel dizzy and lightheaded and short of breath, they lose their balance and are prone to falls and fractures.

It has been reported that almost 17% of the aged population above 65 years are iron deficient anaemic (*Blood* (2018) 131 (5): 505–514).

It has also been reported that around one third of all anaemic older age patients suffer from iron deficiency (*HemaSphere 2(3): p e40, June 2018*).

Iron is the central element of Haemoglobin a protein molecule in the red blood cell which carries the life giving oxygen to all the tissues in our body. A depleted haemoglobin content would severely impair the oxygen carrying capacity of the red blood cells which could be the cause of tissue starvation and even death of the tissue. Ideally, a healthy body contains 12–20g of haemoglobin per 100mL of blood. It was first discovered in 1840 by a German Biochemist Friedrich Ludwig Hunefeld and later in the year 1870 Claude Bernard a French Physiologist discovered the oxygen carrying properties of haemoglobin. It was not until 1962 that Max Perutz and John Kendrew were awarded the Nobel Prize for Chemistry, for the discovery of the three-dimensional structure of Haemoglobin.

Structure of Haemoglobin Molecule

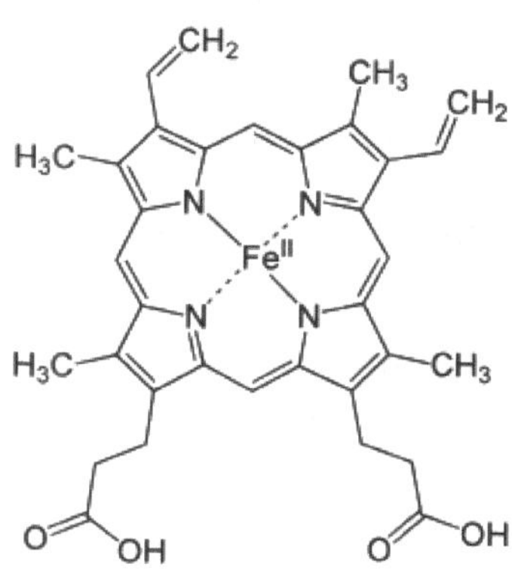

There is another similar protein to the haemoglobin structure with iron in the centre of the protein molecule called myoglobin and is heavily dependent on the availability of iron. This iron containing protein binds oxygen and stores it in our muscles e.g. in the muscles attached to our bone structure, our heart muscle etc. and is specifically entrusted with the task of supplying oxygen to these muscle cells. Very important task indeed for the ageing bodies where muscular degeneration and decay is quite common.

Besides being the central element in haemoglobin and myoglobin iron is an important cofactor in many enzymatic system which are involved in a number of life sustaining biological reactions within our body. As we age the biochemical availability of many minerals such as iron, are, either lost or due to lack of absorption are not readily available and therefore mineral supplementation is important in our old age. It is also important to subsidise the old age diet with iron rich items such as all kinds of meats including the liver, beans (kidney and white beans, etc.), greens like spinach, broccoli, peas etc., foods rich in vitamin C (capsicum, tomatoes, citrus fruits, etc.) potatoes, grains and lentils are good popular food sources.

In this context it must be mentioned that too much iron at any age can be detrimental to health. Common side effects are nausea and vomiting, stomach upset, constipation and stomach or abdominal pain that can be felt if too much iron supplements are taken in an empty stomach.

More serious side effects if larger doses of the supplement are taken over a long period of time can appear as stomach ulcers, liver toxicity as the liver cannot process too much accumulation of iron, accumulation of iron in the brain, toxic effects of iron in the cellular structure; all these if untreated can lead to organ shut down and eventual death.

It is absolutely necessary that people with inherited disease called Haemochromatosis must have medical opinion before even thinking of going on to iron supplementation and /or supplementing their diet with too much of iron rich produce. Haemochromatosis is an inherited disorder, which causes the body to absorb too much iron from food; either from dietary or supplementary intake.

Trace elements: Trace element requirements in our body are in tiny or minute quantities, but nonetheless these are an integral part of our dietary requirement. Most of these are required to regulate our metabolic functions such as in our growth and development, Antioxidant needs, cognitive development, hormonal activities and many more.

The question is, if these trace elements are required in such tiny quantities then are they really necessary or needed in our dietary considerations? Trace elements such as Chromium, Copper, Iodine, Manganese, Fluoride, Selenium, Molybdenum, Cobalt etc. are all essential requirements irrespective of their very minute quantity. In some publications, Iron, Zinc, and Sulphur are also grouped with trace elements, but I prefer not to as these are required in much larger quantities.

The table below provides some information about the trace elements and their usefulness in our body.

(Trace elements and requirements)

Trace Elements	Requirement (RDA)	Daily Adequate Intake (AI)
Chromium	25mg	Not known
Manganese	2.05mg	11mg
Selenium	55mcg	400mcg
Iodine	150mcg	1100mcg
Copper	900mcg	10,000mcg
Molybdenum	45mcg	2000mcg
*Cobalt	6mcg	-
Fluoride	3.5mg	10mg

(https://www.hsph.harvard.edu/nutritionsource/vitamins/ Harvard T.H. Chan School of Public Health, Private school in Boston, Massachusetts)

**National Institutes of Health (NIH) (.gov)*

https://www.ncbi.nlm.nih.gov " articles " PMC4940574

It is noteworthy that different publications have some different requirement amounts mentioned. If these data are to be used for personal nutritional profiling then it is advised that expert opinion from a qualified nutritionist should be sought. Also note there are a few other trace elements which have certain requirements in our body such as Nickel, Vanadium, etc.

Apart from the 10 most popular elements which constitutes our body, there are several other elements which are equally important to our health and well-being. The table below gives some percentage compositions; it is important to mention that certain elements have specific combinations such as oxygen and hydrogen combine to produce water which is the major constituent of our body; our body contains 60-70% water. Similarly, elements like carbon, hydrogen, oxygen and nitrogen combine in variable ratios to produce amino acids and proteins which are the building blocks of our body. There are numerous biochemical such as minerals-enzyme cofactor systems, metallo-organic compounds and mineral binding with protein molecules to form mineral cofactors and many more combinations where minerals find use in our body's biochemical reactions. Some examples are given in the table below.

Mineral Composition of Human Body:

Minerals (Elements	Biological combinations	Biological Functions
Calcium (Ca) Approx. **1.5%**	Oxygen, Hydrogen and Phosphorous	Hydroxyapatite, a compound which is about 65% of the bone structure.

Magnesium (Mg) Approx. **0.1%**	Magnesium cofactors with 300 or more enzyme systems in our body	Role of magnesium in nucleic-acid and protein metabolism
Zinc (Zn) Trace amount	Like Mg, zinc also cofactors with many enzymatic system	In cellular growth, immunity boost and in early childhood development.
Iron (Fe) Trace amount	Iron is the central element of Haemoglobin	Oxygenation of the blood, DNA synthesis.
Potassium (K), Sodium (Na), Chlorine (Cl), Phosphorous (P) Approx. **1.5%-2.0%**	Most of these elements (K and Na) act as electrolyte combining with Cl and P	Intra and extra cellular fluid balancing the osmotic pressure to preserve cellular structure
Oxygen (O) **65%**, Hydrogen (H) **10%**, Nitrogen (N) **3%**	Oxygen and Hydrogen combine to form water	More than 60% of Human body composition is water
Carbon Approx. **18%**	Carbon combines with O, H, N to make carbohydrates, amino acids proteins etc.	Amino acids and Proteins are the building blocks of our body
Sulphur (S) Approx. **0.2%**	Also required in the biosynthesis of essential amino acids, proteins and many other bio-active compounds	Sulphur is important component of all cell structures and is essential for the growth of all living organisms.

Cobalt, Selenium, Copper, Iodine Trace amount	In very small quantity Less than 0.1%	Manufacture of red blood cells, antioxidant activities, and catalytic activities in several enzyme systems.

In the Table above of the Mineral composition of the human body, I have attempted to give a very basic understanding of the minerals required in our body. The biological combinations referred to are the most important combinations e.g. oxygen and hydrogen from water, which is the most important combination in our body. Apart from this oxygen and hydrogen also combine with various other elements such as carbon, nitrogen, silicon etc. to form many important biologically active and useful compounds which are required for the growth, maintenance and health of our body. Compounds like amino acids, proteins, carbohydrates, enzymes, hormones and many more compounds which not only provide the body with strength and vitality but also keeps our body powering on. In fact almost all of the bio-chemicals in our body doing various tasks to keep our body healthy and biologically functioning are composed of not only the major elements as in the table A but also several other trace elements Chromium, Manganese, Molybdenum, Silicon, Fluorine, Iodine Copper and many more. These elements are required only in tiny amounts and participate as cofactors for many enzyme systems to perform biochemical reactions to keep us going. Our life sustainability depends not only on the major components of our body but also on other elements irrespective of how minute requirements are for these trace elements.

It is interesting to note that out of so many elements in nature our body uses around 20-21 elements), but only 4 of these make up around

95% of our body composition. We can classify all the elements used in our body composition (according to *Mark Belan "The Elemental Composition of the Human Body" published June 27, 2022*) as the Main Elements, Essential Elements and Trace Elements in the order of their percentage utilization in our body. According to the author:

The main elements (Oxygen, Hydrogen, Carbon and Nitrogen) occupy almost 96% of the total body mass which means on a 70kg body these 4 elements occupy bit over 67kg. This is mainly due to the combination of oxygen and hydrogen to form water which is the highest component of our body; anything above 60%. The rest of these elements are used in making up compounds of biological significance e.g. proteins amino acids, enzymes, carbohydrates, hormones and numerous biochemical that our body utilizes daily. These elements are the front-line elements without which there would be no human body.

The essential elements, in this category there are 8 elements which are Calcium, Magnesium, Sodium, Potassium, Chlorine, Phosphorous, Sulphur and Iron. These essential elements make up around 3% of the body composition. All are important e.g. Calcium and Phosphorous are integral element in the composition of our framework the skeletal structure. Iron is the central element of haemoglobin. Sodium, Potassium, Chlorine, Phosphorous are important for our electrolyte make up and also for our cellular integrity and structure.

Sketch pf Human Skeletal Structure

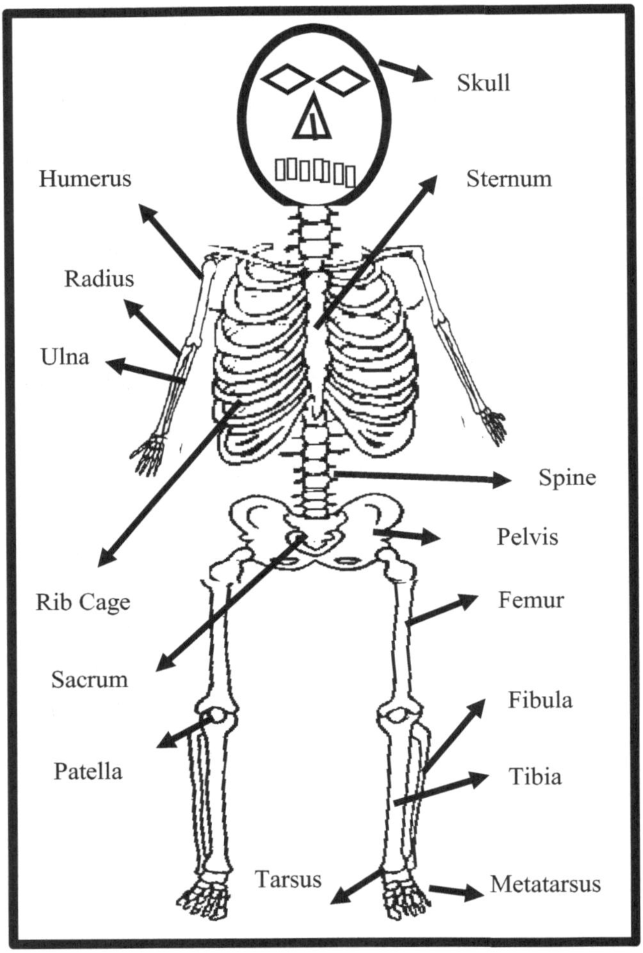

Human skeletal structure is a bony framework which supports our posture and upright stance. This framework is held together by connective tissues, cartilages, ligaments, and tendons to hold the bones and muscles together in proper configuration and format. Any loosening of the connective tissues can be detrimental to our structural framework and posture.

The integrity of our skeletal structure starts to weaken with age as the connective tissues lose their flexibility due to degeneration of the protein collagen and elastin and become stiff and harder such that they do not flex as easily as in younger days resulting in difficulty in movements, friction between bone joints causing pain and also instability resulting in trips and falls.

Weaker bones result in skeletal structure diseases e.g. arthritis, loss of bone density, osteoporosis and osteopenia, fractures etc. and other complications resulting in lesser quality and quantity of bone marrow and red blood cell production.

To keep the integrity of our skeletal structure health as we age, we must intake plenty of calcium and vitamin enriched food and also additional supplements if required. Your general practitioner or advice from a registered nutritionist may be necessary in some cases.

Include dairy products milk cheese yoghurt etc. in your diet. Regular exercises and mild weight training (do not exceed your capacity) also help. Avoid falls and avoid putting unnecessary pressure on your joints especially knees and elbows if they are already weak, work to reduce extra weight on your upper body to minimise additional pressure which can be from your additional body weight.

Medical interventions and regular medical appraisals are also good management regimes for keeping on top of your skeletal structure health and wellbeing.

Vitamin C: It is generally assumed that in a well-balanced diet, the availability of vitamin C may be adequate. But, there are a number of issues to consider before this general perception can be assumed to be applicable.

Adequate mix of fresh fruit and vegetables and other food supplies which are known sources of vitamin C.

Cooking process if the food needs to be cooked prior to consumption. Since vitamin C is thermos-labile meaning heat sensitive cooking for too long at a significant temperature can destroy the vitamin C content and the food may be rendered useless from vitamin C content.

Food preparation prior to consumption is also very important as vitamin C can be easily oxidised, is highly water-soluble and does not store well in food supplies (ref. Table below). Raw food rich in vitamin C must be prepared prior to consumption either raw or prepared by cutting, blanching and washing. Each step depletes the level of vitamin C. Some people prefer to peal the skin of the fruit and vegetables which are concentrated in nutrients in some cases more so than the body of the produce itself.

Why is vitamin C important for us?

The answer is quite complex. Many important nutrients are not as essential as vitamin C as they can be biosynthesised in our body. But we humans and several higher primates cannot due to a missing enzyme unavailable to us in our body due to a genetic disorder. This is common in all human beings irrespective of our individual characteristics such as where we come from what our food source is and differences in our physical attributes.

Most animals can bio-synthesise vitamin C in their body from glucose which is the primary food molecule, but we cannot due to the missing link an enzyme called **L-gulono-1, 4-lactone oxidase**. Hence we require a daily intake of vitamin C to perform numerous tasks within our body directly or indirectly. Vitamin C is involved in countless tasks within our body, too numerous to count.

In the words of Dr. Emanuel Cheraskin, Dr. Ringsdorf and Dr. Sisley

in their Book THE VITAMIN C CONNECTION (Harper and Row 1983) write,

"There are more than ten thousand published scientific papers that make it quite clear that there is not one body process (such as what goes on inside cells or tissues) and not one disease or syndrome (from the common cold to leprosy) that is not influenced directly or indirectly by vitamin C."

Imagine, this was in the early 80's, so now the publication count must have surpassed 100,000 publications. It is the most common essential nutrient which has also been the most studied among all other known vitamins. Every day something new is being discovered or discoveries made to consolidate existing theories and uses as scientists and researchers are discovering new bio-functions of this wonderful vitamin. Starting from its anti-oxidant activity to its use in fighting pollution and heavy metal poisoning within our body and recently its role in anti-ageing has elevated the status of vitamin C as the most daily supplemented nutrient.

There are many publications on this subject, those who are interested can look up the following references for bedtime read. K Akhilender Naidu, Vitamin C in human health and disease is still a mystery? An overview. Nutrition Journal 2003, 2:7 Vitamin C Edited by Jean Guy LeBlanc.

As suggested above there are several food sources which have significant amounts of vitamin C. Here are 10 most common food items:

Please note these data are picked from published data scattered over the internet. I have also included a reference on data published by *Dr. Liji Thompson https://www.news-medical.net/health/Sources-of-Vitamin-C.aspx*. Which is noteworthy.

Vitamin C content greatly varies on the soil condition, the environment of the growing zone and several cultivation procedures. It is therefore important to consult your nutritionist when preparing a dietary intake programme.

Some of the everyday food sources of vitamin C:

Among vegetables, commonly consumed red peppers, cabbages, tomatoes, broccoli and Brussels sprouts provide a significant portion of vitamin C. Other sources are potatoes,

spinach, green peas and some beans provide the moderate amount. It is generally assumed that due to nutritional depletion in aged population availability and processing of vitamin C from food in the body can also be depleted and hence the need for vitamin C fortification greatly increases.

(Approx. vitamin C content of some fruits and vegetables)

Food Source	Vitamin C levels
Citrus fruits e.g. Limes, Lemons, Oranges, Mandarins, grapefruit etc.	50 -80mg/100g (Lime and Lemon have slightly less)
Cabbages	Approx. 50mg/100g
Broccoli	Approx. 65-90mg/100g
Black Currents	Approx. 180mg/100g
Papaya	Approx. 60mg/100g
Garden Tomatoes	Approx. 25mg/100g
Potatoes	Approx. 20mg/100g
Carrots	Approx. 5-10mg/100g
Parsley	Approx. 130mg/100g
Green Capsicum	Approx. 75mg/100g

Vitamin D: Vitamin D is an important nutrient for our old age which essentially helps absorb calcium from the food.

It is also known as the sunshine vitamin because it can be bio-synthesised through our skin using the sun rays.

It is generally assumed that due to nutritional depletion in aged population, the availability and processing of vitamin D can be significantly impaired and hence the need for vitamin D fortification by means of daily supplementation. Also, diminished exposure to sunlight and the reduced availability of 7- dehydrocholesterol (7-DHC) on the skin's dermal layer as we age reduces the capacity of the skin to convert sun rays into vitamin D. Furthermore, weaker liver and kidney functions as we age also causes the vitamin D production and processing to be impaired.

There are several functions of vitamin D which are closely linked with the health of elderly people:

Vitamin D is important in maintaining the skeletal structure and for the prevention of osteoporosis in the elderly.

Vitamin D has a significant role in the improvement of brain and cognitive function in elderly people; it also improves the depressive state in the elderly population (*Ref: Nutritional Therapy and Metabolism. 2011; 29(1):8–21; Clin Interv. Aging. 2013; 8:509–14*).

It has also been reported in several reputable publications that Vitamin D has positive benefits in old age diseases such as osteoporosis, cardiovascular impairments, type 2 diabetes, hypertension, cancer and immunity (*Ref: J Aging Gerontol. 2014 Dec; 2(2): 60–71*) also published in *https://www.ncbi.nlm.nih.gov " articles " PMC4399494*).

For those above the age of 70 should supplement regularly and around 500-1000 IU (international units) of vitamin D daily; if unsure check with your local general practitioner or physician.

As I have mentioned, the elderly population in any community suffers from a vitamin D deficiency. According to the Australian Bureau of Statistics (National Health Measures Survey; NHMS), it is very likely that due to the supplementary intake of vitamin D the elderly population (65-74 years old) rate of deficiency is only 15% but the rate increases to 20% or over in elderly citizens 75 years or over (*Ref: https://www.abs.gov.au/articles/vitamin-d*).

It is also reported that approx. 44% of the elderly male population and 26% of the elderly female population are Vitamin D deficient; (*National Institutes of Health (NIH) (.gov)https://www.ncbi.nlm.nih.gov " articles " PMC6178567.* This work was presumably done in Canada.

Conversion of Sun's Rays into Vitamin D

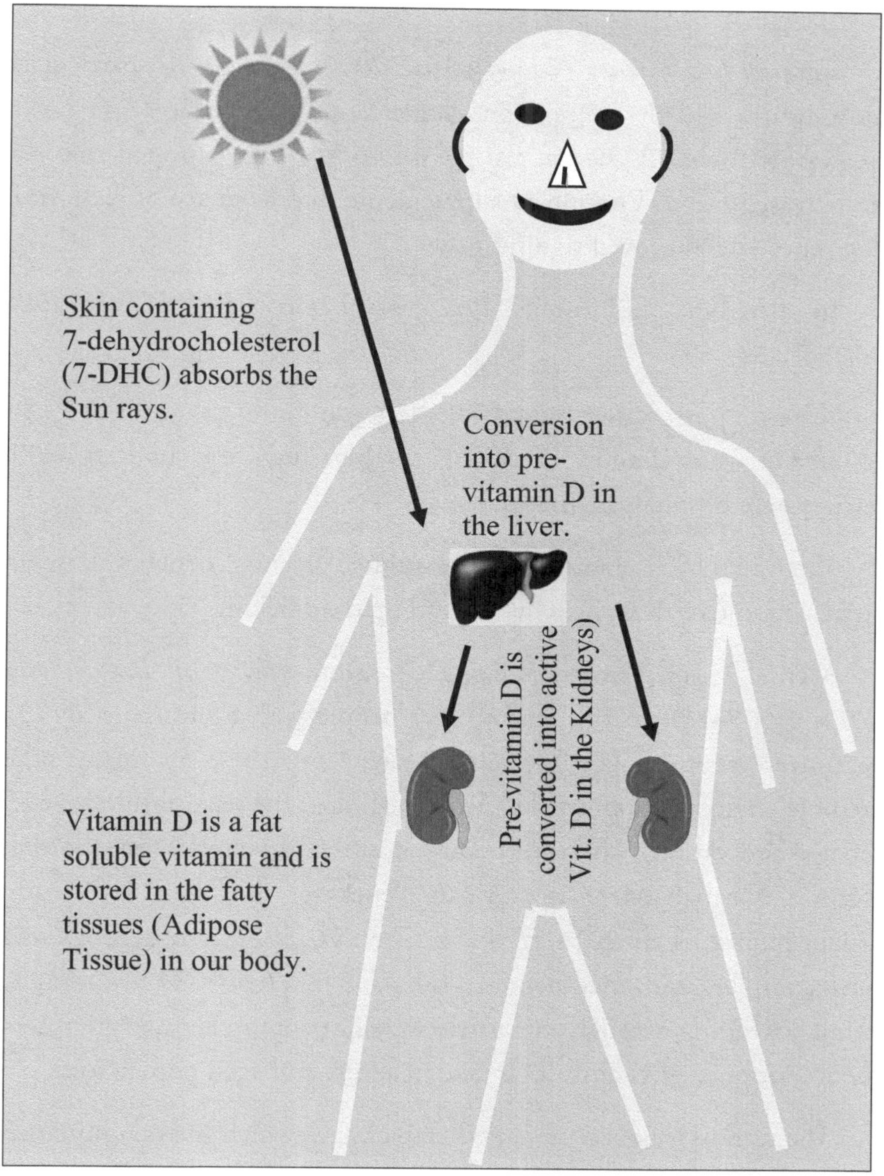

According to a survey/study in 2007 it was estimated that there were about 1 billion people in the world in 2007 or earlier who were vitamin D deficient (Ref: Holick MF.

Vitamin D deficiency. N Engl J Med. 2007; 357:266–81, particularly most of the elderly population globally are susceptible (*Ref: J Clin Endocrinol Metab 2009, vol. 94 pg. 1244-50*). It is expected that due to increased use of Vitamin D supplements the incidence of vitamin D deficiency has improved significantly.

In a recent publication (*Ref: Turk J Endocrinol Metab. 2022; 26(2):79-84*)

It was reported that out of 706,434 adult subjects studied 57.8% (408,882) were vitamin D deficient. This study was undertaken in tertiary care hospitals in Turkey.

Vitamin D has many clinically studied positive benefits in senior citizens; some of those benefits are summarized below.

Mental Health Problems e.g. Depression: (*Ref: Clin Interv Aging. 2013; 8:509–14*). In this study, older people with a mean age of 73.8 years were found to be Vitamin D deficient. There are many other credible references published which have linked the relationship between old age and various aspects of mental health and neurological disorders. Authors Meghan Meehan and Sue Penckofer in a very informative article published in 2014 (*J Aging Gerontol. 2014 Dec; 2(2): 60–71*) have compiled and documented "The Role of Vitamin D in the Aging Adult". Reading through the article we get a comprehensive glimpse of the importance of vitamin D intake in adults and aged population.

The authors have also presented a table below which gives a summarised understanding of the vitamin D and benefits in older population.

Vitamin D Deficiency and Diseases in the Aging Adults:

(Ref: Table used from J Aging Gerontol. 2014 Dec; 2(2): 60-71)

Cognitive Decline
Associated with cognitive decline Associated with ↑ risk for dementia Associated with ↑ risk for Alzheimer disease Mechanisms may include inflammation and formation of amyloid plaque in the brain
Depression
Associated with major depression Associated with ↑ depressive symptoms Mechanisms may include neuro-immunomodulation and regulation of neurotrophic factors in the brain
Osteoporosis
Evidence for ↑ risk for low trauma fracture Associated with ↑ risk for falls Mechanisms include ↑ PTH and bone turnover
Cardiovascular Disease
Associated with ↑ risk for cardiovascular morbidity and mortality Associated with ↑ stroke in women Mechanisms may include smooth muscle proliferation and inflammatory processes
Hypertension
Associated with ↑ risk for hypertension Mechanisms may include alterations in the regulation of the renin-angiotensin system
Type 2 Diabetes

Associated with higher fasting glucose levels Associated with ↑ risk for insulin resistance Potential mechanisms may include insulin sensitivity and secretion
Cancer
Associated with ↑ risk for colorectal cancer, more specifically rectal cancer Associated with ↑ risk for metastatic prostate cancer Potential mechanisms may include alterations in the autoimmune response and cellular proliferation

Vitamin D is one of those nutrients (such as Vitamin A) which if not taken appropriately and within a therapeutic dose can cause more harm than good. Over-dosing can cause hypercalcemia meaning too much of the element calcium in the blood stream causing renal failure and impairment in kidney functions. It can also cause an imbalance in electrolyte equilibrium and loss of salt from tissues and cellular structure. It can also cause hyperparathyroidism, and joint aches and pains. Other conditions are the formation of calcium stones, and calcium plaques in the artery walls causing irregular blood pressure. Also, too much calcium built up due to vitamin D toxicity may cause some problem with bone structure and the skeletal structure upon which the human frame or the gait is based on.

Vitamin D poisoning occurs almost exclusively from excessive supplementation rather than sun exposure. While outdoor activities are generally safe in terms of vitamin D, prolonged sun exposure can still cause sunburn, so protection is advised.

The most common symptoms of vitamin D toxicity are:

Nausea and vomiting.

Dehydration and increased thirst Weakness in muscles and skeletal structure, pain and discomfort felt during movements Often fatigue and tiredness are felt in the body Besides these common symptoms, other major symptoms can be observed, e.g., cardiovascular issues, confusion and disorientation, etc.

With a sensible management plan vitamin D toxicity can be treated and the recovery percentage is high, especially with younger patients. With older patients recovery can be a slow process. There is a moderate incidence of serious complications.

The research study Referenced above (*Turk J Endocrinol Metab. 2022; 26(2):79-84*) also reported that vitamin D toxicity (Hypervitaminosis D) was detected in 5.5% of all the adult subjects studied; and of these subjects, almost 6.5% were 70-79 years age bracket and 6.6% were above 80 years old. A significant number indeed. The results published are quite comprehensive and subject to further interpretation and confirmation. I feel that the higher rate of Hypervitaminosis D in older people is due to non-compliance of medicine intake and also insufficiency in vitamin D metabolism and a lack of bio-usage of accumulated vitamin D in the fatty tissues of the older age people.

Preparing for the Ageing Lifestyle:

It is not an easy transition to make into the senior lifestyle let alone into the mid-senior to matured senior ageing bracket. Consideration must be prioritised not only from the health and fitness consideration but also from the various lifestyle change adaption point of view.

Let us firstly consider the changes and sacrifices that are needed to adjust and accommodate transition into matured senior years.

Attitudinal shift, decreasing self-reliance with increase in the level of dependence, changes in socio-economic considerations, crisis management, preparation for any contingency plans are some of the considerations that really need to be worked out prior to reaching a stage where a mature senior experiences helplessness and trauma of getting old.

Ageing is inevitable and there is no means to turn back the clock. Life can only go forward, how pleasant the journey will be depended on how well one has set a well thought out plan in motion for the future years.

Attitudinal shift: As we grow old, and retire from active duties and lifestyle we tend to be more withdrawn and closed off. In many countries and communities old age is seen in a very negative light. A feeling of prejudice and discrimination shown towards older people can often weigh heavily on them pushing them further into despair. Unfortunately, the ammunition to fight back is missing due to a lack of confidence and, dependence on others. The shift in attitude in older people makes them vulnerable. How can this be changed? Educational activities to enhance the value of elderly people and to dispel any negative attitudes and sentiments can go a long way to bring the intergenerational gap closer. The elderly in the community are blessed with life experiences and values which have been acquired from years of experience. These elite groups are repositories of knowledge and wisdom and the younger generation can only benefit from exchange of ideas. People from the older generation must have a positive outlook towards their own attitude, although it is easier said than done it seems that negative attitude plays heavily in the background. Ageing is associated with loss of independence, loneliness and decreasing social contacts, general health and well-being and importantly socio-economical standing. All these contribute to the attitude. Those who can overcome some or all of these negative attitudinal contributors have a good response in ageing gracefully. In developed nations, there are programmes that to some extent assist in uplifting self-esteem and therefore steer the attitudinal shift in the positive direction. Aged people in poorer nations where there is no or very little assistance available are prone to age more rapidly with often dire consequences.

Self-realization: This is a strong motivator and potentially can guide elderly people to overcome many negatives in life's journey. I see that there are three major scopes that may help.

Social bonding……… When we get old and transiting to a life much different from our former life's activities, such as living in a complete retirement, living alone or in an old-age home or housing facility, progressive delineation in health condition, decline in sustained available funds and generally in a withdrawn state of lifestyle, ageing can then set in quite rapidly. The first and foremost thought should be to put up a defence so that we can protect ourselves from the negatives of the ageing process.

How can we do that?

Not easy of course!

Amongst the ageing population are those who feel ageing is a curse and in fact I have heard people commenting along this line and thinking that as they are now getting old they do not have the power to contribute to society and perceive themselves as a burden to the society, they are more susceptible to age quickly and experience a significantly higher level of stress and trauma which shortens their lives causing misery and hardships. They have given up the will to age gracefully and to lead a meaningful life.

With all the negatives around linked with ageing it is primarily up to us to challenge ourselves in charting our course to pave the path to live healthy, live within our means and to restore confidence, self-esteem and dignity. These comments are mainly directed at the ageing population in poorer countries where aged care support is almost non-existent.

Improvements can be made through collective enterprises, social networking, educational and various other activities and implementations which rekindle the power and passion in like-minded seniors. You will be surprised how quickly word spreads and soon there will be groups forming canvasing seniors' health and well-being, idea exchanges in the senior's social network, senior's voice and power of persuasion and many more positive activities groups and collective idea flow for the betterment of seniors. All it takes is a group of people with leadership ethics, not strict leadership enforcement to improve the general social structure and status. Again this is a thought for seniors in less advanced nations.

Another important point of consideration is mentoring programmes. Many seniors by virtue of their past experiences socially or through work experiences have gained knowledge and skills which they can share amongst each other or pass it on to younger generation to close the intergenerational gap and secure wider acceptability within their community.

It is very encouraging that the United Nations General Assembly has devoted this decade (2021-2030) to "Healthy Ageing" by collaborating with Governments of many nations to improve the general health conditions of seniors globally. World Health Organization (WHO) is also actively involved in trying to resolve common health conditions in seniors. Let's hope that this effort by the world bodies can help seniors live healthier lives and live relatively happily and comfortably.

Certain facts about old age diseases:

For general discussion we are mainly concentrating on the following old age diseases and health complications.

We are limiting our discussion to the elderly population over 65 years old, there are exceptions and many seniors live to the ripe old age of 90 years and above enjoying good health and general well-being. Our statistical information is taken mostly from observations of the **Centre for Disease Control and Prevention** (CDC) which is US based health and wellbeing *operating arm of the Department of Health and Human Services.* Although, Food and Drug Authority (FDA) and CDC both work under the health jurisdiction of the US Government their charter remains different and independent of each other.

Let's look at the some of the most common old age health complications globally; the items are not based on any priority of importance. Needless to say, all old age diseases and health complications must be looked at with similar importance.

The % is based on old age population (65+ years) both based on US and Australian data comparison.

Also, note these data provide valuable references as to both male and female seniors (65+) and highlights the need for periodic health checks in both categories of our elderly population. Risk increases in every category with age and at the age of 85 or more a significant number of elderly citizens are reported to be affected. Data presented in the table is collated from various reference points from the internet, a few of these references from where the data are extracted are mentioned.

(Ref: The National Council on Aging (NCOA) https://www.ncoa.org " article " the-top-10-most-comm. Statista https://www.statista.com " ... " State of Health Australian Institute of Health and Welfare https://www.aihw.gov.au " health-disability-status Australian Bureau of Statistics (www.abs.gov.au " statistics " health " latest-release, Centre for Disease Control and Prevention (Gov.) www.cdc.gov> fastats>older american-health.

Common Old Age Health Complications:

Disease Category	% Male Population	% Female Population
Cardiovascular	20% (Australian) 20% (US)	12% (Australian) 13% (US)
Obesity	83% (Australian) 42 (US)	73% (Australian) 46 (US)
Depression	12% (Australian) 16% (US)	11% (Australian)
Chronic Kidney disease	26% (Australian) 25% (US)	17% (Australian)
Diabetes	19% (Australian) 27% (US)	12%(Australian)
Arthritis	39% (Australian) 35% (US)	55% (Australian)
Longevity	82yr (Australian) 82 yr. (2023 data)	85yr (Australian) 85 yr. (2023 data)
Lung Disease (COPDS)	7% (Australian) 10% (US)	7% (Australian) 13% (US)
Dementia	3% (Australian)	5% (Australian)
Hypertension	35% (Australian)* 67% (US)	34% (Australian)* 74% (US)

*Age 65-74 (Australian Bureau of statistics (2022–23).

Chapter 6

AGE CARE AND RISK MANAGEMENT

"With age may come dependence, just as others once depended on us. But there is no room for self-pity—only room to live well and look ahead."

– Jay Das … (2024)

Caring for others can pose a great challenge not only to the caregivers but also it is a self-challenge for the care receiver.

The questions being asked are what are the risks involved and where can things go wrong?

Institutionalised care can be more challenging as there are set of rules and guidelines by which institutions provide care. These challenges are more complicated when these institutions are audited on a regular basis (if not they should be) and a report on the outcome is produced based upon which the care institutions are graded.

Risk management is a well-practised procedure in many industries. It is an important procedure by which assessments can be made for both safety and quality control systems that are in place and used in day to day routine practices. In health care and patient care situations, it can be a handy tool for the audit of how the care regime is managed and enforced. It validates accountability of the operating procedures in place and justifications there-off and determines the needs for resetting the procedural systems in operation. The most important objective of risk management is to learn from the procedural deficits which underlines risks to patients, in this case seniors so that every seniors who are being cared for are look after well and most of their needs are met with.

All risk evaluations case by case deserve careful consideration and where possible must be addressed and prompt remedial action taken. Unfortunately, due to lack of funding private or governmental often causes the system break down resulting in sufferance by the senior's concerned ending up in grave situations.

In institutionalised old age care risk assessment points can be too numerous for the scope of this book and must be handled delicately by experts in the field. However, for the sake of our own understanding and awareness following can be commonly identified.

Staff ratios and inadequate training

seem to be a major issue. This is an important factor as fatigue and lack of understanding of the specific care needs can put patients at risk. Frustrations and dissatisfaction among the caregivers often results in anger and loss of patience resulting in diminished quality of service and welfare of the patients. This is indeed sad as I believe old-age care workers must be equipped and trained to handle elderly and infirm patients with dignity and plenty of understanding. Some seniors requiring Palliative care or Hospice are at the end of their journey and deserve the utmost dignity and peace.

Also, we all, not just the carers should appreciate that seniors requiring any type of care are there due to their inability to conduct their daily activities independently and are unable to understand health care instructions or are too slow, so, remember "patience is our virtue".

Nutritional and care needs of seniors

is of paramount importance and is often neglected. Providing two main meals

Is not just enough, especially when the food quality is sadly lacking. It is understandable that due to cost restraints and bottom line pressures, mundane repetitive meals are provided which an elderly senior often rejects and ,or, partially consumes. This creates inadequate supplementation leading to depletion of nutrient needs. The end result is manifested in continued diseases with prolonged recovery time. Often with serious health consequences.

If possible serving of a mix of variety of foods from the five main food categories e.g. Fats and Proteins, carbohydrates, Fruits and Vegetables, Cereals, Nuts and Legumes and Dairy products is essential to a healthy dietary intake. Where needed a daily supplementation of a multi-vitamin and Mineral is also a good thing. This fulfils the daily vitamin and mineral needs of an elderly person and tops up their daily nutrient needs.

Then there is inadequate consumption of fluids. Dehydration is a common cause in old age care, be it institutionalized or home care. It is around 51% for institutionalised care and 41% for home care (*Res Gerontol Nurs 2017 Nov 1; 10(6):260-266*).

The total daily average requirement of fluid intake is around 1500-2000 mL. Water is an important commodity, more like nutrient for all living beings on our planet. Water constitutes around 60% of our body weight. Losses due to dehydration can have serious health concerns for all living beings, especially in the older population. This is more so for the elderly who are on heart medications and diuretics and hot sweaty days. Disorientation, confusion, loss of balance and many anatomical and physiological factors are at play which severely affects their health and general well-being. Continuous neglect in water or fluid administration may lead to death.

Fall and trip protection

for elderly people who lose their balance and steadiness with age can be a critical issue. Risk minimization procedures can be put in place in various ways. Placement of handrails in strategic locations e.g. toilets, washroom facilities, and common areas where seniors frequent is a good start. Living areas can also be made clutter-free free and hard surfaces can be lined with carpets and other softer alternatives so that damage due to falls or trips can be minimized. Special needs and protection of seniors who are known to suffer of Sarcopenia, Osteoporosis and Osteopenia should be of prime consideration. Adequate supplementation of higher doses of Calcium, vitamin D etc. may also be considered if required.

Sensory perceptions

such as loss of hearing and sight may need to be compensated for by use of external aids e.g. hearing aids and spectacles. However, responses to touch, smell and taste are some of the other sensory perceptions that a senior may lose sensitivity to resulting in a decline in their quality of life. These are quite important with health implications and where possible a remedial action should be considered.

My thoughts on this matter is quite simple and clear. A decline in sensory perception in the elderly may cause injury; for example, a reduced sensitivity to touch may cause loss in temperature and vibrational detection and therefore result in burns in touching hot surfaces, lower thresholds to climatic temperature fluctuations may cause physical discomfort. Reduced sensitivity may often be a cause of ignoring wounds and pains due to sprains or in extreme cases fractures which if not attended to timely can have serious health implications in vulnerable seniors. Decline in smell perception can often be a hazard to seniors for example a lower threshold to smell sensitivity can lead to smoke, petrol fumes, poisonous gas inhalation etc. It is up to us to take adequate precautions and safety measures in care residences, seniors independent, home or community care establishments to minimise or better still total prevention of such dangers.

There are several other factors and considerations that come with a care regimen, the most important are psychological and emotional abuse and often physical abuse. It is reported *Elder Abuse in Australian Aged Care Facilities inside Ageing https://insideageing.com.au "elder-abuse-in-Australian-... 21 Dec 2020*) that around 39% of elderly living in aged care institutions in Australia have experienced some form of neglect, emotional or physical abuse. This is well above the documented statistics of around 10% of aged care residents in Nursing homes in America according to National Centre on Elder Abuse (NCEA).

Globally, in a 2017 report of a survey of 28 countries the abuse of 60+ aged people was 1 in 6 (almost 15.7%).

Abuse of older people World Health Organization (WHO)

https://www.who.int " Health topics 15 June 2022.

These statistics are a lot to be desired and offences often go unreported. In many situations there are no risk management procedures in place to deal with such offences and the perpetrators go on with repeating these offences time and time again.

It is very important that risks of such nature be identified and handled swiftly and perpetrators put out of action where they can do no further harm. A continuous risk management procedure to address this must also be put in place and regularly monitored.

Recently I came across a report (Elderly abuse in India – The Hidden Truth, Dignity Foundation *https://www.dignityfoundation.com " elder-abuse-in-in...*)

The results were staggering; the result of a survey of 22 cities in 2022 found that 35% of the elderly suffered abuse from their own sons, 21% from their daughters-in-law; and 2% from their house help who were not related. Abuse ranged from both psychological and physical violence. The abuse and neglect does not seem to have reduced with time as previously reported statistics (conducted in 2014) suggested that almost half of India's elderly (50%) experienced abuse; the sad part is that these abused elderly identified 77% of their abusers as a family member.

I am sure in recent times in modern developed India situation has improved and authorities are taking action as swiftly as possible and within the framework of current protection laws for the welfare of their elderly citizens.

Elderly abuse and neglect is a very complex issue arising out of a lack of knowledge and information available. Many elderly are powerless and often frail and disoriented coupled with lack of literacy and complete dependence upon their carers (community care or in-house care) that they feel obliged to keep silent in fear of any repercussion and reprisals. It is sad but I guess that's the way it is and seniors are the sad suffers.

In, home-based care at least in Australia and America and several developed and developing nations the care given by the carer usually a family member is more conducive to the comfort and well-being of the seniors usually parents, grandparents and other elderly relatives intimately associated with the family and the house hold. There are external agencies (NGO's) and government departments specially set up for this where help and assistance can be made available. Often brief respite for the carers and also home help is available to give them temporary relief from the stressful day-to-day care regime of the elderly under their care. I admire those people for their dedication and sacrifices.

It is my general opinion that in societies where life flows at a slow and steady pace and demands do not outgrow the needs, a more harmonious cohabitation can exist. Such was life in the previous centuries when the urge for "what they have got I must have too" sentiment was well under control. This is quite prevalent in poorer rural communities, where caring for elders is still a social and moral duty.

Nutritional and clinical interventions

should be mandatory in every care plan be it institutionalised or home-base. There are certain daily nutritional needs that seniors under care must be provided with depending on their health status. It is widely recognised that seniors need certain fulfilment in their lives. I being a senior myself and somewhat still an active person my first and foremost consideration will be to preserve my independence and dignity. These are the two most powerful considerations in our life that keep us looking forward to the future. Other things such as living healthy and self-sufficiency are adjunct to our longevity and our well-being. Many seniors living under care have to compromise to the extent that there is a balance and a compromise between the care-giver and the care-receiver.

A lot to think about. But then unfortunately there are seniors with frailty and infirmity with a high degree of dependence who require specialised Nutritional and clinical Interventions. Care regime for these helpless seniors are more involved and more complex and a well thought out care plan must be instigated.

Common Nutritional deficiencies and requirements for seniors who are home based or institutionalised must reflect their nutritional profile. This can be done clinically and, or, via assessment of their physical status. For example, daily calcium and vitamin D supplementation may be required in most cases of seniors with advancing age. It is also important to realise that frail seniors can often lose balance often resulting in falls and fractures. This is aggravated due to Osteopenia and Osteoporosis.

I am of the opinion that prevention is better than cure, often cure comes too late. I therefore believe every senior above the age of 60 must have an initial bone density scan followed by a regular intake of calcium and vitamin D supplementation. The dosage can be established clinically after a medical consultation. Milk, cheese, yoghurt and other calcium-rich dietary intake is also an important consideration and gives additional protection with age. It is estimated that globally more than 43% of adults aged 50+ have Osteopenia which can develop into Osteoporosis if not intervened at the early stages. It is also important to realise that our calcium needs are increased with age and especially the requirements in female seniors are more prevalent.

In various sections of the book, we have raised the issue of supplements in the elderly population. But for the sake of clarification and simplistic understanding in the context of the supplementary needs in our ageing seniors let me again raise those issues in brief and with more specificity.

Vitamins and minerals, why are they needed: Vitamins are essential as supplements for all ages. In seniors more so as our anatomical and physiological performances start to slow down. These essential nutrients are important for our body to sustain life and stay healthy.

Vitamins act as biological catalysts regulating and enhancing numerous life-sustaining biochemical reactions e.g. our cellular metabolism, energy-producing reactions, cellular repair mechanisms and many more. They are essential as our bodies cannot manufacture them or do so in too little quantity. Therefore all vitamins have to be supplemented or must be delivered in sufficient quantities so that our biochemical reactions are efficient and effective.

In brief there are a few notable biological functions that vitamins perform in addition to their main functions as biological catalysts.

1. Certain vitamins assist in lowering the risk of infection;
   Vitamin C, shortens the severity and duration of cold and cough infections.
   Vitamin D, is important in boosting our immunity and immune functions.

Vitamin E, protects against rancidity of our fatty materials e.g. lipids which may cause infection due to these fats breaking down into reactive toxic oxygen species (ROTS) in the body.

Vitamin A, fights infections and keeps it at bay to protect our immunity.

2. Maintenance of healthy hair nails and skin;
   B vitamins are known to do just that and many more; they are also important to keep our nerves and nervous system healthy and functioning efficiently.
3. Cognitive improvement:
   Several vitamins in combination with minerals help boost our memory, our alertness and mental functions.
4. The functions of vitamins in our body are too numerous to enunciate individually but just to mention a few; vitamin K assists with blood clotting which helps stop bleeding in wounds and cuts, otherwise, we could bleed to death. Vitamin B12 is important in producing and regenerating new blood cells. Folic acid (vitamin B9) and is important in pregnancy and the development of the foetus.

Minerals are also very important in our daily existence. I have developed a chart so it can give the readers a simple visual and a quick reference. The chart is by no means complete as there are several other elements which in their own way are important to our health and well-being. Next charts provide some insight on the function and their food sources.

(A Brief Vitamin and Mineral Chart)

Vitamin A: For healthy eye and vision, healthy skin and immunity

Vitamin B Complex
A group of 9 vitamins B1, B2, B3, B5, B6, B7, B8, B9 and B12. Helps in growth and development. Energy production cycle, hair skin and nails.

Vitamin C: Immunity boost, antioxidant activity and iron absorption in the body from food

Vitamin D: Immune functions, regulation of dietary Calcium from food, hormone regulation etc.

Vitamin E: Fat soluble vitamin, protects body's stored fats from rancidity

Vitamin K Blood clotting and coagulant activity

Calcium: For healthy, teeth and bone structure. For healthy muscle and nerve tissues. Regulation of muscle and heart functions.

Magnesium: Important for muscle and nerve functions, sleep and relaxation, enzyme-cofactors.

Zinc: Zn is important in our DNA and protein synthesis, wound healing and immune system.

Iron: Constituents of Haemoglobin and Myoglobin and transportation of Oxygen to lungs, heart and body tissues

Trace elements:
Selenium
Manganese
Copper
Chromium
Iodine
Fluorine
And few others

Co-factors in many enzyme systems, energy producing reactions and as regulators of Oxidation-Reduction Mechanisms.

Sodium
Potassium
Phosphorous
Chlorine

→ These elements among other functions preserve the cellular integrity by keeping the osmotic pressure balance between intra and extra cellular fluids across the cell membrane. Also these elements form the electrolyte group regulating fluid distribution in our body.

Some food sources (Vitamins)

Vitamin A

Liver, eggs, dairy milk cheese, fish and fish oil and many other yellow/orange fruits and vegetables e.g. carrots, pumpkins mangoes and also fresh spinach.

Vitamin B complex (9 B - group vitamins)

Dairy products, whole grains and cereals, fresh fruits and vegetables broccoli, avocados, mushrooms asparagus, spinach watermelon.

Vitamin C

Fortified fruit juices, citrus fruits, fresh greens spinach, broccoli

Vitamin D

Sunshine vitamin from sunlight, egg yolk, and fatty fish oils, Mushrooms, milk and dairy products.

Vitamin E

Seeds and nuts, wheat germ and sunflower oil, pumpkins, asparagus, avocados, mangoes

Vitamin K

Fresh Green vegetables lettuce, spinach, collards. Turnips, broccoli, eggs and soya beans.

Often a food source may not result in desired effect. Storage, preparation and cooking conditions are important for the nutrition value of the produce.Remember fresh is best

Some food sources (Minerals)

Calcium (Ca)	Magnesium (Mg)	Zinc (Zn)	Iron (Fe)
Milk and dairy products are the best source of Ca. Also, seeds including poppy, chia, sesame, celery are also good. Green leafy spinach, kale, collard etc. Rhubarb and oily fish salmon and sardines are a good source.	Seeds, nuts, legumes, whole grain, fatty fish, banana, avocado, leafy green vegetables all offer significant levels of Mg.	Shitake mushrooms, seeds and nuts, eggs, whole grains, dairy milk and cheese, animal protein are all good sources of zinc.	Red meat, liver and kidneys, shell fish oysters and clams, green vegetables spinach and broccoli, seeds pumpkin, quinoa, legumes kidney beans chick peas etc. are all loaded in iron.

Electrolyte Elements (EE)	Trace elements (TE)
Electrolyte elements sodium, potassium, chlorine and phosphorous are widely distributed in our food source e.g. banana, oranges tomatoes, strawberries, avocados, milk and dairy, beans, potatoes, broccoli, meat products etc. Again a wholesome meal is a good source.	Cocoa, dark chocolates are an excellent source of (TE). Seeds, nuts, beans, milk and dairy, leafy greens are all good sources. In general a wholesome meal provides healthy portion of TE.

The Trace Elements are only 1% of our body composition. These 9 or 10 elements if you also consider Nickel, are required in day-to-day life-sustaining activities in microgram quantities.

A microgram is one-thousandth time of a milligram which is one-thousandth time of one gram, so you can imagine how tiny and minute these quantities are which are used in a significant number of biochemical processes within our body every moment of the day to keep us alive.

These trace elements are Zinc, Copper, Chromium, Manganese, Cobalt, Selenium, Iodine, Fluorine, Molybdenum and Nickel.

Our body is a composite machine which functions efficiently without fail when all the components of our body is in harmony and working in unison.

Clinical interventions in the elderly are challenging due to an array of complications that may require specific attention and so the carers in institutionalized or home care situations must have the basic training or access to clinical care facility as soon as the situation requires. Risk minimization plans in these circumstances must be in place and often drilled to coordinate to the effectiveness of the operating procedures. Mimicking a reality and triggering the emergency plan is also a good risk mitigation qualification. Evaluation of the success by scoring the performances of the active participants is a highly motivational and remedial exercise and prepares for the real thing if and when it may happen. In institutionalised care, the facility should be periodically audited to check for the preparedness of staff and functionality of the equipment in place. Home-based care facilities may not require a rigorous procedural audit due to several uncontrolled environments and as these facilities do not render themselves to any clinical intervention. Even though, caring for an elderly person will have risks that need to be addressed and mitigated. For example, the foremost requirement is to have a medical intervention procedure handy which allows a quick call to the ambulance or other patient transportation vehicles for relocating the patient to an adequate medical facility. Provision for simple first-aid procedures etc. Assuming all the basic care facilities are in place it is important that the primary home carer must be mindful of the following requirements. Adequate hydration requires providing the seniors with plenty of water or (suitable fluids) at periodic intervals. If the seniors are not under 24/7 care regimen then they should be left with adequate fluid dispensed in various handy location for the senior to access. Limiting salt, sugar, fatty foods and other unnecessary food additives in a senior's diet is important, so that food is easily digestible but also palatable to improve portions for consumption. We all let alone seniors get sick and tired when a dietary food served is repetitive and bland. Mixing and matching from the 5 food categories often serves the best purpose both in terms of food value and acceptance. Food should be enjoyed. Seniors suffering from irregular bowel movements and constipation must be served with dietary fibre adequately. Access to a balanced diet from the five food groups would contribute to a healthy lifestyle leading to a reasonable health and mental state of the seniors and will help them age gracefully.

A good diet plan, mild exercise and social interactions are key to longevity and improved life span.

Finally we should also look at a senior's nutritional needs. This is in addition to the nutritional contribution a good diet plan offers.

It is reported that seniors with advancing age require vitamins, minerals, fibres, essential fatty acids, protein etc. to fortify their body's nutrient pool as they get depleted by a myriad of reasons such as effect of medication, digestive and nutrient absorption issues, renal complication and a number of health conditions that they suffer at their late stage in life. To counteract that a good quality of multi-nutrient supplement must be included in their daily food and nutritional intake. Some of the nutrients mentioned above can be obtained from their diet plan but others must be supplemented.

Seniors with independent living should be mindful of all the above issues discussed as their contingencies are similar to either the institutionalized or home-based care. In addition to several others they are responsible for their health and well-being. However, the issues that they must be aware and take note of are discussed in the following paragraphs.

Independent living is a better and a more dignified choice where a senior can decide for themselves, knowing that help is at hand should there be a need for it; but a contingency plan for at-call external help must be kept handy.

Self-help seniors must keep a close watch on the following: Their nutritional needs, a diet of balanced meals and additional supplementation.

When organising meals seniors must consider a wide mix from the 5 different food groups and also vitamins and minerals fibres and also omega-3-fatty acids.

Regular hydration including a clean glass of water at appropriate intervals of time.

Digestive issues and bowel movements must be considered as this has a significant effect on their health.

Participation in social activities will boost their self-confidence and improve their physical and mental status.

Avoid the use and abuse of Alcohol, Tobacco and Drugs as these could over time lead to health and mental cognition decline.

In many instances cooking a meal is not on the menu for many seniors. In these situations, external meal services may be called for. There are a number of senior-friendly meal services that can organise meals for needy seniors in conjunctions with their nutritional needs. These meals can be well balanced, portion-controlled and pre-cooked for convenience and a senior has only to heat them up prior to consuming. This also, takes away a lot of worry and stress from a senior's mind.

Chapter 7

THE ESSENCE OF AGEING GRACEFULLY

"Life is like a river—sometimes rough, sometimes smooth. As we age, we flow gracefully toward our maker, like the river meeting the sea."

– Jay Das 2025

The essence of ageing gracefully is a philosophy and a way of life that all seniors must practice irrespective of their age and lifestyle. It needs certain lifestyle changes, discipline and positivity in their lives which can provide enormous benefits with every passing of time units. It is more fulfilling and gives us seniors a sense of achievement and enhancement in our status and self-awareness.

Looking after our physical body and mental state can only be a good thing, so we all can enjoy a better living be it in a family situation, socially or communally; we feel good and hopefully live happy, healthy and a longer life.

Achieving fulfilment in later life often takes a few adjustments and a willingness to change. But, many seniors at this stage of life tend to become complacent, resistant to change, and are much attached to their familiar routines. Their approach to life can sometimes feel mundane, and the prospect of altering long-held habits may seem stressful or even daunting.

As a result, many seniors simply "live as she is and as she goes" until the end. I say "she" not out of gender bias, but in reference to the well-known old English naval phrase, *steady as she goes*, traditionally used by a ship's captain to maintain course.

My view is that, there are 8 major steps we can follow as depicted schematically. At least these are my tip:

My Tips for Ageing Gracefully

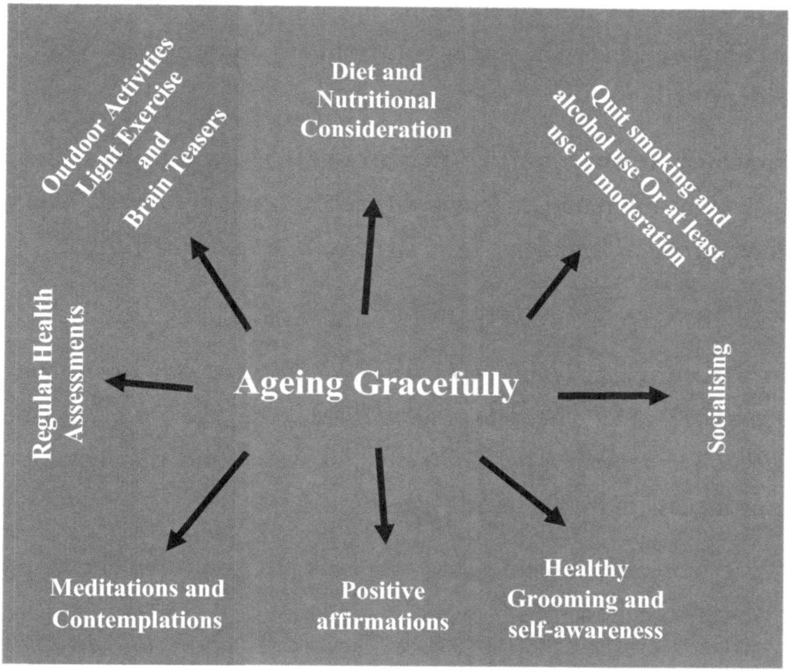

It is inevitable that as we age, we slow down and begin to take our daily routines for granted. Yet, by adopting some of the tips above, life can become more fulfilling and enjoyable. Simplify and adapt these ideas (as shown in the schematic diagramme) to suit your lifestyle, there's no need for drastic changes. Take it step by step, at your own pace. As the saying goes, *"easy does it."* Sit back, embrace the process, and enjoy the journey. Ageing gracefully can be truly uplifting. It brings out the best in us "seniors" and gives fresh meaning to life and living in our later years. Of course, it's easier said than done but the rewards are worth it.

Most important ingredients for ageing gracefully are good nutrition, exercise and an active brain. If and when you have incorporated these in your ageing process, then, it becomes a way of life. It is to some extent true that our genetic makeup has some influence on our longevity, but it is not pre-destined. It is an emerging science and very complex in nature as the common genes which may contribute to our longevity have yet not been identified.

Previously it was estimated that around 25% of our life span can be influenced by our genetics (*Is longevity determined by genetics? MedlinePlus (.gov) https://medlineplus.gov " ... " Genetics and Human Traits*).

It is, however, an estimate only.

In a recent study (*Bodywork: What role do genes play in our longevity? Oklahoma Medical Research Foundation | OMRF https://omrf.org " 2023/08/08 " bodywork-what-role-do...*) it was found that genetics may account for less than 7% of our life span.

So, let's breathe easy and if we can look after our own ageing process then we can age gracefully.

Diet and nutritional consideration:

Diet and nutrition are both equally important for our healthy ageing. Good food means good nutrition. And, good nutrition is important for general health and well-being. Good quality well balanced dietary intake can provide us with proper nutrients, e.g.,

Carbohydrates for energy.

Proteins for essential amino acids for our tissue repairs, assist in muscle wastage and muscle wear and tear repairs and also energy production.

Minerals for strengthening our skeletal structure.

Vitamins for activating and participating in various biochemical reactions happening within our body.

Without these, our daily existence could be in jeopardy.

Good nutrition is like putting good clean fuel into a machine for its optimal operations. Poor and substandard food intake can cause serious disruptions to our health and longevity which may manifest into disease conditions which if not medically intervened may end up in serious life-threatening situations such as certain types of cancers, cardiovascular diseases, diabetes, pulmonary disease etc.

Healthy eating is associated with a lower risk of serious health issues.

Consuming bad food (Junk foods) with substandard nutrition has a direct link with our anatomy and physiology insofar as putting the organs and their functions at risk.

(Reading reference: *Fast Food's Effects on 8 Areas of the Body Healthline https://www.healthline.com " health "fast-food-effects-...).*

Fast foods or junk foods are appealing to consumers due to taste enhancement by excess addition of sugars, salts, fats oils and proteins carbohydrates and many useless fillers or bulking agents e.g. cellulose.

Admittedly, it does not happen overnight but over the time sub-standard and low quality food intake has been shown to be quite detrimental to health and efficient functioning of our organs. There are many examples of such incidents; let me mention just a few. However, please note these do not happen overnight but have accumulative effects over a period of time.

Eating too much oily and fatty foods can cause fatty deposits in several organs. Main concerns are fatty liver, fatty arteries also known as Atherosclerosis, excessive body fat deposits and also fatty lungs (Lipoid pneumonia) and many more.

Excess fat circulating in our circulatory system due to excess dietary intake can be deposited in any part of our body including our vital organs. This is known as toxic fat

(Visceral fat) and can be very harmful to us and cause obesity leading to several diseases.

Excess sugars in our dietary intake lead to cellular and tissue overloading causing type I and 2 diabetes and endocrine dysfunctions such as pancreatic overload causing a lack of or slow insulin production.

Leaky gut syndrome, irritable bowel syndrome and many other digestive system diseases can be caused by food poisoning, food allergies, incomplete digestion of the ingested foods loaded with unwanted excipients amongst other causes such as infections, the effect of ingested medication stress lack of hydration and others.

Periodic or controlled fasting

can be a good thing provided it is planned on some basic characteristics of the senior who is fasting and some basic principles of good nutrition. The question to ask yourself is what am I going to get out of the fasting and is it right for me. So, let's look at some important considerations.

Adequate hydration requirement is met.

Do not let your body starve such that it has to resort to utilizing your body's stored fats in order to extract energy to keep your vital systems functioning.

Fasting is not intended for frail and infirm seniors.

Your BMI must not be at the lower end of the table based on your height and weight.

Unless you are obese, do not use fasting to reduce your weight. Think of fasting as a cleansing process that helps to eliminate accumulated toxins from your body. There are a few other considerations which must be addressed individually before undertaking routine fasting.

There are a few ways of fasting one which is performed over 24- a longer period of time and the other is intermittent fasting which considers eating between main meals (e.g. binge eating) by reducing the portions and frequency of intake in periodic gaps determined by the person fasting. This frequency or the gap in between meals is variable and should be adjusted for minimum discomfort.

Intermittent fasting in my opinion is the best fasting way for us seniors and if weight loss (unless you are obese) is not of prime consideration then it could provide a lot of health benefits. Always remember before undertaking a fasting plan it is absolutely necessary for seniors to have a medical opinion on your suitability for fasting and must consider your medications as a priority. However, please note that intermittent or any kind of fasting can be harmful if you have an underlying medical condition.

One final word, after commencing fasting a periodic medical assessment is necessary on your health condition and if need be alteration to the fasting plan may be necessary.

What are the benefits to be had from intermittent fasting?

From what I have read up fasting seems to be quite safe for seniors unless there is an underlying health issue. But in general carefully planned intermittent fasting can be a good thing with several health benefits.

A research finding from the University of Florida (*Intermittent fasting leads to significant weight loss, slows aging ... UF Health - University of Florida Health https://ufhealth.org " news " intermittent-fasting-leads-s...*)

reported that intermittent fasting can assist with weight loss and several other physiological functions, slow the ageing and disease processes. Further health benefits are associated with

Weight Loss
Lowering of LDL
Lowering of risk of heart diseases
And many more.

It is generally recognized that a 16/8 fasting programme is most suited for seniors, however this programme can be adjusted according to the health advice and the comfort and doable level of the senior.

A 16/8 intermittent fasting programme involving a 16 hour fasting after eating within an 8 hour window in a 24 hour daily programme. For example eating between say 10 am - 6 pm and fasting for 12 hours after i.e. 6 pm till 10 am next day.

Outdoor Activities and Light Exercise and Brain Teasers:

Outdoor activities and exercise is a great way to keeping fit. Any amount of activity including light exercise is beneficial and a cause for improvement in their health condition. But as a guideline, a 30 minutes brisk walking will set you in motion. According to the CDC (Centre for Disease Control Prevention) 30 minutes of moderate activity such as aerobics, muscle-strengthening, bit of weight training, gardening, yoga and any brisk activity can all be excellent choices. Mixing and matching to avoid repetition can really be the activity to improve the physical and mental health of all seniors 65+. Socialising, dancing and the very many outdoor activities e.g. hiking, swimming, and bike riding are also important and increase your choices and preferences.

To improve brain activities and alertness we can form groups and play cards, chess, and some board games or if alone can try card game such as solitaire, pyramid or patience. Other choices are scrabble, puzzles and word games. Improvement in both physical and mental health, fitness and alertness helps boosts the level of confidence and overall wellbeing. It helps us to enjoy our lives more, reduces isolation and loneliness and prepares us to deal with our chronic and debilitating diseases better. It also improves our posture and steadiness and reduces the risk of trips and falls which do have serious implications and can render us inactive for a considerable length of time.

Quit smoking and alcohol: Quitting the so-called unhealthy practices e.g. smoking, alcohol abuse and frequent use of recreational drugs can be harmful and can leave us with a long-lasting health and mental issues which not only can ruin us physically but mentally and financially as well and push us deep into social isolation and loneliness. It is very easy to get tangled in this web in our early senior hood when we still think that we are resourceful and can handle all eventualities that live can throw at us. But these are meant to lead us on to the point of no return unless we are mindful of the future consequences and get out of the web at the earliest with professional help. These are facts with reality checks with very sad endings.

Drink in moderation if you must and socially, know your limitations, discipline yourself and stop when you have to.

Regular health assessments: Regular health and wellbeing checks will not only allow you to go steady on your life's journey but also knowing that you are doing all you can to keep healthy will give you mental peace and happiness to chart your future course of action with some ease and peace of mind. May be you were hesitant in taking the trip that you wanted for a long time but were not certain of your health and well-being and kept pushing back for another time; but now you can with a relative confidence.

Just a few preliminary clinical tests such as blood tests, Urine tests for biochemical markers for any underlying diseases, and examination of your stool may reveal any abnormal findings in your bowel and gastro-intestinal tract area (GIT) and periodic blood pressure monitoring can reveal quite a lot about your health. It is never too late to arrest any health issues that may be at hand rather than to leave it in a too-hard basket to deal with later which may be a bit too late.

Modern medicine also has other tools such as various scans and measurements that can also get into the inner depth of your body to reveal any issues needing any immediate medical intervention.

Meditations, contemplations and positive affirmations: It has been long known to mankind that meditation is a powerful tool to reduce our stress and anxiety levels. It improves among many positive mental attributes, self-awareness, self-esteem and emotional stability. All these factors are essential for healthy ageing. Scientifically it has now been well documented (*J Alzheimers Dis. 2015; 48(1):1-12.*) that meditation improves performances on neuropsychological tests when conducted on people with age-related memory loss.

Mental clarity, memory boost and attention spans can also be improved through meditation.

Further reading reference (*12 Science-Based Benefits of Meditation Healthline https://www.healthline.com " nutrition " 12-benefits-of-...*).

After reviewing many credible reports I have concluded that although Meditation, Contemplation and Positive Affirmations are not tangible science and therefore no solid proof can be derived from the findings the trio still has the power to reflect a positive influence on our inner-self and self-realizations. They wittingly or unwittingly have the ability to challenge our mind and soul and fill them with positive thoughts and belief and sets us on our future path of positive outlook on life. Very powerful ingredients indeed to Ageing Gracefully.

Healthy grooming and self-awareness:

This is also important, how you look is how you feel. If you look good well-groomed you feel great beaming with self-confidence and self-esteem. This does not mean you need to go to a hair dresser weekly, or to a tailor or a seamstress or just browsing through dress shops searching for new clothes. Not at all, do with what you have got and attire choice-fully to suit the environment and the climate. Maintain proper and regular hygiene, apply your favourite cosmetic make-ups lightly so that your own skin shines through.

For those in a communal living and or home-care situations it is important for the carer to be considerate of their dignity and independence to the nth degree and preserve their familiarity so that the seniors under their (carer's) care. Older seniors can very easily become anxious and stressful if there is too much of a change in their routine and familiar environment, so carers must be mindful and be respectful of their (seniors) wishes and emotions.

Seniors hygiene and grooming has both psychological and physiological benefits;

As mentioned earlier it helps boost self-esteem, awareness and confidence.

It has a positive effect on mental health and well-being.

It gives a relaxed feeling, reduced stress and a sense of pride.

It improves social and cognitive skills.

It can also increase immunity and improve overall health and general well-being.

It may lower the risk of dementia, uplift spirit and improve moods.

(*Ref: The Lancet Neurology. 3(6), 343-353, June 2004 and Psychology Today 2016, Jun 30*).

Another important step is that it offers seniors a more independent lifestyle and social interactions fully knowing help is there if needed.

Decluttering and down-sizing:

This sounds irrelevant and useless but when referred to in the context of ageing and age related circumstances suddenly its relevancy becomes highlighted and significant.

So, what does it involve and what are the benefits. There are two oppositional pulls at play here; one, sentiment for which many of us oldies are known for. We love our possessions for their sentimental values. The other, is I believe in the following steps as a start. The first step is to lower our expectations; go for only what we need and not give in to our wants. There is no end to our wants and if we can control our wants or unwanted desires we can progress into the other steps.

Our next step is to charter our destiny. Where do we go from here? Worldly possessions are like hobbies to pursue when we have the time, means and inclination, but in our old age our health and well-being is the number one priority. Memories are wonderful, they remind us of our past. Photographs and some tangible objects in my opinion are enough to cling on to rather than our materialistic possessions and memories generated from those possessions which can in many ways clutter our judgement and normal active memory.

Possessions may bring comfort to us in our old age, but at the same time it can be a burden. Our worldly possessions or our materialistic possessions can be a cause of our mental anxiety and stress as it can brings a constant stream of worry and insecurity of losing them. Research has shown that there is always a possibility of some old age people get into a hoarding disorder (HD syndrome) which can cause a lot of agony and distress, which is exacerbated when those possessions are forcefully disposed of for whatever reasons there may be, health and hygiene reasons, accommodation issues etc.

Democritus (born: circa 460 BCE and died about 370 BCE) an ancient Greek pre-Socratic philosopher once famously quoted "Happiness resides not in possessions, and not in gold, happiness dwells in the soul".

This is what Ageing Gracefully should be; it is a journey that all seniors with reasonable mobility and a positive attitude to life can traverse, navigating the course through social interactions, a holistic approach to life, self-assertiveness and happiness as true to Dali Lamas teachings "The purpose of our lives is to be happy". It is a natural progression through various stages of our life and ending in the most important stage enriched in wisdom, grace beauty and dignity.

Chapter 8

AGING GRACEFULLY "THROUGH A HOLISTIC LENS"

"Aging gracefully begins with holistic care—when body, mind, and soul age in harmony. It's not just about living longer, but living with depth and humility, purpose, and meaning."

– Jay Das
(January 2025)

After completing the chapter on "The Essence of Ageing Gracefully" I felt compelled to add this final chapter to emphasize that graceful ageing is not about just flowing in the current of the ageing process but to bring about a balance cultivating our physical, mental and emotional, social and spiritual parameters. From when we are born to approaching the end in our life cycle, many priorities are set and change. But, one thing remains constant within our mind and psyche; how to make this journey of ageing more dignified and comfortable. It is a universal transition and as the author of this book I had to ensure that this final chapter offered both practical strategies and wisdom looking at the ageing process through a holistic lens.

The entire book has been structured in a way that it will provide some good information and knowledge to prepare seniors and others who are planning on making the transition into their senior years to better map out the course of their life's journey. Because believe me, the journey in understanding the ageing process can be a complex and lonely one.

There are many facets that have been included from where the readers can get an understanding of human life cycle to the end stage of our life when we need assistance and caring and the feeling of dignity and security. Attempts have been made to address aging process from multiple angles, including biological, psychological, social, and practical aspects. Now, reading on through this chapter I am hopeful that the readers particularly the seniors will be better prepared to understand and navigate the challenges and opportunities that come with ageing. Additionally this final chapter will allow readers to understand the complex nature of ageing while offering actionable tips for how they can embrace it gracefully.

Holistic approach gives further perspective into the role of a family and community, application and assistance of technology in ageing process, mental health and alertness, cultural perspectives and many other factors of relevance which lends an interesting point of view and can offer practical guidance to make our ageing journey much more comfortable and meaningful. Although bits and pieces from the above mentioned points have been included throughout the book in different contexts but when brought together it provides a meaningful area for discussion and considerations and adds a further dimension to the Essence of Ageing Gracefully.

The role of family and community in aging:

In human society a family plays an important part from our early development from childhood to our senior years. It makes us feel connected and gives us the sense of belonging. We establish our roots and connections which in most case are permanent binding, a common thread which binds all family members loosely or strongly. A senior in the family feels more secured and supported as they age. Now as the trend for seniors to live in our homes are becoming more common perhaps due to certain reasons e.g. socio-economic reasons, affordability of institutionalised care facilities, decline in several areas of care such as funding –cuts all point out to a favourable decision for home living and home care. This is certainly a more economical alternative and certainly a more comfortable approach to a dignified age-care living. Although having said this a time comes when institutionalized and – or palliative care becomes necessary.

The role of a family becomes important and I do not consider this as a burden to a family as their monetary outlay if any is quite minimal since the parents or grandparents choose to stay in their own dwellings and endeavour to use their own savings or governmental assistance in the form of an old age-pension or other financial assistance. This is also a preferable mode of operation for governmental bodies as their outlays have been shown to be significantly less. From a reported source on Govt. Services 2024 Part F section 14, Aged Care Service report Home Care expenditure vs. Residential Care it seems that in Australia govt. spends about 57.7% for Residential Care while for the Home Care the expenditure is around 33.5% and other aged care services, including flexible care, workforce and service improvement, and assessment and information services around (8.8%). This comparison is for Australian Aged care population. From a literature search it was also evident that the US government spending in the aged care sector also points to a similar trend as by the Australian government.

Application of technology in ageing:

We live in technological age where the use of smart TV s, mobile phones and digital media dominates almost all aspect of our lives. Every bit of information required to live our daily lives are easily accessible and retrieval of information is quite simple in many cases. Search engines such as Google, Yahoo, Ask.com and many others are at our figure tip to provide at least some working information which can be useful and get us over our immediate requirement. Mobile phones are tools to keep in touch with friends and family and essential services are just a phone call away.

Let us now look at some of the area that modern technological advancements have made our live as senior citizens more comfortable and helping us in our quest for living gracefully.

On line shopping (OLS); this has created a tremendous opportunity for all of us young and old alike. By ordering our requirements on line and getting it delivered to our doorstep has significantly minimized risk factors for our elderly citizens. Just naming a few OLS has minimized the risks of accidents, trips or falls, carrying shopping loads thus minimized instability and other risks. Admittedly some social jurisdictions in advanced countries may offer shopping day outs etc. but largely OLS provides our seniors sense of security and quality free time to spend at home and do the chores they love e.g. gardening or just light walks or socializing. There are many more flow-on and benefits and usefulness of OLS.

Cognitive improvements:

This is really worth noting as on line searches can provide quizzes, brain teaser games, general knowledge to improve our awareness of our surroundings, around the country and internationally. There are different levels of games and quizzes which one can access to according to their competency. As we are accessing these games and quizzes at home in our privacy there is no harm done and failures can only strengthen our wits. These days there are audible books which can be accessed to for book lovers who due to failing eyesight had given up on their passion for reading. Also accessible are news items in the form of local and international news prints, senior's magazines and journals which can get them up to speed as to the senior's world.

Mental health and physical alertness:

World Health Organization (WHO) has estimated that the aged population of the word will exceed 1.4 billion by 2030 (one in six) and by 2050 this number could be as high as 2.1 billion. These numbers are high by any standard and the governments of various jurisdictions must start planning from now to provide adequate services if they were to have any chance of success. Sadly enough it has also been reported that around 14% of the aged population 60 years and above live with some sort of mental disorders (Institute of Health Metrics and Evaluation. Global Health Data Exchange (GHDx). (https://vizhub.healthdata.org/gbd-results/, accessed 20 October 2023). It is an overwhelming issue that we all should be concerned with and where possible help out in our own way. Social isolation and loneliness are major contributors together with abuse of older people which in many instances go un-noticed. There are a wide range of abuses from physical, verbal, psychological, sexual, financial abuse, and neglect. It is reported (Yon YY, Mikton CR, Gassoumis ZD, and Wilber KH. Elder abuse prevalence in community settings: a systematic review and meta-analysis. Lancet Glob Health. 2017; 5(2):e147–e156) that one in six older adults experience abuse, often by their own carers. Abuse of older adults has serious consequences and can lead to depression and anxiety and often ends up in tragedy. Indeed a social injustice and a blight on our society which we all must remedy not waiting for authorities to take action which may lead to further delays with serious consequences. Although, the subject of abuse and mental issue in aged population in almost all jurisdictions are paramount and scope for specialist interventions, it is important for the community at large to be aware and assist the victims and report perpetrators to the law enforcement authorities.

As a community we can be more vigilant and observant of the ageing process of our family members, friends and neighbours and act responsibly and respectfully to support the situation. But before we do that we need to be able to recognize and understand the changes we all go through at various stages of our lives; so that we are able to offer any assistance.

What are the most common changes we go through as we get old? Here are the 6 or so visible and physiological signs of old age symptoms. Some of these changes or symptoms have already been discussed in the earlier sections of the book.

- Physical; hair and skin appearance changes which are a strong reminder that we are ageing. For example greying of the hair and sagging and/ wrinkly skin.

- Sensory perceptions; a decline in our sensory perceptions in particular sight and sound are yet a strong indication that we are entering into the 7th stage of our life (Ch. 1).
- Cognitive impairment; as in delayed processing of information by our brain.
- Irregularity in Metabolism; which impacts our digestive and nutrient assimilation capabilities which results in a consistent lack of energy.
- Anatomical and physiological decline; this can have a wider health implications in elderly people during ageing process and can affect a range of impairments in various body systems and organs.
- Psychological effects; in elderly people can be devastating and cause a lifelong trauma with no apparent cure.

In aged people the consequences can be slow but progressive and in most cases the effects are irreversible.

(Systems in Our Body and Consequences)

Systems	**Main Organs**	**Fundamental actions**	**Consequences**
Cardio-vascular	Heart, blood Vessels and blood	Circulation, a supply chain of oxygen and nutrients.	Weakened heart, blood pressure fluctuation
Immune	Thymus, Spleen and Lymph nodes	Fight infections	Prone to frequent infection, longer healing times

Musculo-skeletal	Bones, Muscles and Joints	Support body structure and provide secure framework for our organs	Weak body framework and loss of steadiness, easy trips and falls, muscular aches and pains
Respiratory	Lungs, Bronchi and Respiratory tract	Body's purification system and waste disposal.	Collapsed lungs, insufficient supply of Oxygen, toxicity build up
Nervous	Brain, Spinal cord and Nerves	Body's communication network.	Loss in body's communication network. Mental confusion
Renal	Kidneys, Bladders and Urethra	Body's waste disposal and blood filtration	Fluid retention, toxin build up
Gastro-intestinal	Stomach, Gastro-intestinal tract food	Body's food processor. Converts ingested food into nutrients for the body	Malnutrition, dehydration
Integumentary system	Body's largest external organ our skin	Body's climate controller. Protects body from injury, external microbial infiltration.	Loss in body's temperature control, weak protective barrier

Endocrine System	Pancreas, Pituitary Pineal glands.	Regulation of Body's function Steroid and Hormone production.	Effects growth, reproduction body's metabolism

As we embrace a holistic approach to aging, it is essential to assess the issue comprehensively. A care plan should be tailor made and designed to address the full aspect of a patient's needs, rather than serving as a temporary fix for immediate concerns. I have identified eight key points that can significantly influence a holistic care regime.

Let's look at it diagrammatically

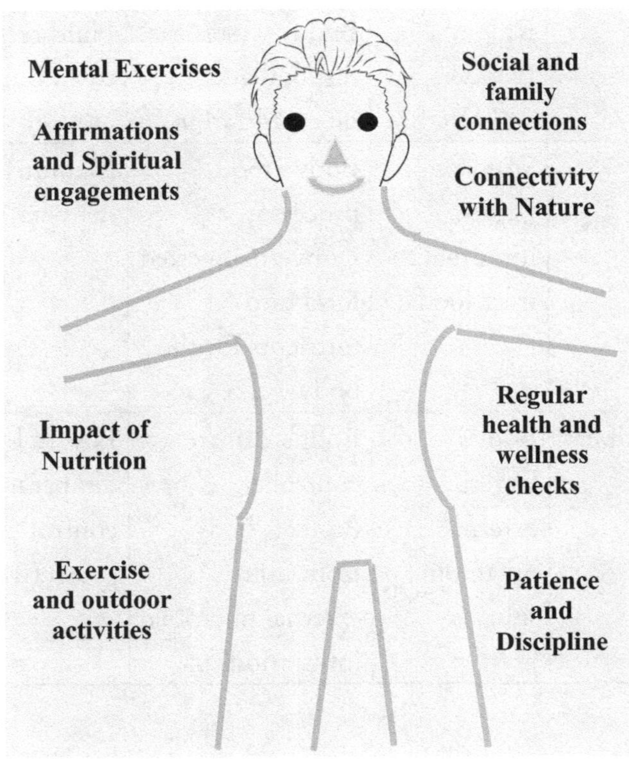

- Mental Exercises in ageing process can be very
- Mental exercises; doing regular mild brain teasers then progressively graduating into more complex form of quizzes, solving puzzles, card games etc. can be a good way to sharpen ones wits and keeping the brain active. It also helps healthy sleep patterns and boosts cognitive functions.
- Social and family ties are absolutely important in our old age. Connecting with close social groups creates positive bindings and keeps loneliness at bay. This is a definite step forward towards happiness and longer healthier life.
- Affirmation and Spiritual engagements have been shown to have positive effect on our wellness. Some science backed publication e.g. Sherman et al., 2009; Critcher and Dunning, 2015.

  Self-affirmations affect brain activity (Cascio, C.N., and et.al. social cognitive and affective neuroscience 2016, 621-629). There are many other examples which are science backed published in various scientific journals.

  Spiritual engagements have also been associated with many positive effects in the lives of elderly people; just a couple of science backed references are quoted for those who are interested in studying further. Balducci L. Geriatric Oncology, Spirituality, and Palliative Care. J Pain Symptom Manage. 2019 Jan 1; 57(1):171–5. Blaber M, Jone J, Willis D. Spiritual care: which is the best assessment tool for palliative settings? Int J of Palliat Nurs. 2015 Sep 2; 21(9):430–8.
- Connectivity with Nature has an overall beneficial impact on the wellbeing of senior citizens. According to an article in Nature (www.nature.com/articles/s41598-020-74828-w) it has been reported that simple activities in the 24-week therapeutic horticulture intervention proved positive in several areas of wellness. These were Cognitive improvements, sleep hygiene, Psychosocial and Physical outcomes and general happiness parameters. Participants were retired and were

of Chinese ethnicity and females 70 years plus of age. Researchers concluded from this study that structured nature based programmes can have significant positive benefits in improving the physical and mental health of senior citizens.

- The impact of nutrition in the process of ageing is very significant. Generally there are 3 types of nutrients; macro-nutrients, micro-nutrients and others. Let us re-define these with specific examples and their utility. Macro-nutrients are nutrients which the body needs in larger quantities. Such as Proteins, carbohydrates fats etc. Their specific role is to provide the body with energy. Micro-nutrients as the name suggests are required in a smaller quantity, but none the less their role is quite specific and important. This class of nutrients are essentially vitamins, minerals. Micro-nutrients must be supplemented in our diets or taken regularly as daily supplements. Their function within our body is to maintain growth, immunity, brain activity and many other of our bio-chemical reactions which are essential to keep us alive. For example our cellular metabolism will be impaired if our body did not have sufficient B-group vitamins and certain minerals. Lack of certain micro-nutrients will disable our body to bio-synthesise several enzyme systems, hormones and other bio-chemicals which are important for our body. Glaring examples are Iron the central element of haemoglobin which carries oxygen to our brain and all cells and tissues. Insulin, a hormone which neutralizes excess sugar in the blood. Imagine deficiency of iron and lack of pancreas's ability to produce insulin would be devastating to our normal living. The other class of nutrient I call are natural and nature identical ingredients which in their own right have therapeutic benefits and often act as adjuncts together with essential nutrients. Some examples of these are bioflavonoids which occur naturally in fruits and various plant based foods. Due to their anti-oxidant and anti-inflammatory actions they were also known as vitamin p, however, technically they are not classified with the mainstream vitamins. The other example is inositol which is often referred to as vitamin B8; again like vitamin p it is technically not a vitamin but an adjunct. It helps relieving symptoms of several mental disorders, metabolic syndrome lowering of cholesterol, and many other health conditions. Also included in the others category is Probiotics which are known to support and promote a healthy gastro-intestinal tract (GIT) population of good bacteria. This has a positive benefit in restoring GIT health and also has a significant positive effect in the immune response in elderly people.

- Regular health and wellness checks are important for an early detection and intervention of disease condition and state of an elderly patient. Australian Govt. Dept. of Health and Aged Care recommends annual checks so that a meaningful dialogue is initiated to explore the history of patients' health condition and a holistic care plan can be triggered. This is an insurance that elderly adults stay well and healthy from both physical and mental point of view.
- Exercise and outdoor activities are very many at our disposal from mild walking to rigours workouts. Although I doubt very much that an elderly adult will feel comfortable in undertaking regular heavy gym workouts. The choice should be based on preferences, enjoyment and within the comfort zone of the elderly subject. I prefer a mild workout combining weights and free hand exercises of up to 30minutes max. There are several references and start-up programmes for seniors to get into and graduate to something more appropriate if they so choose. Regular exercises offer huge benefits of physical fitness, stability of the posture resulting in less trips and falls.
- Lastly, I believe that patience and discipline are essential, as they help us face the challenges of aging with grace and dignity. As we grow older, our wants and needs naturally begin to decline, and we are encouraged to find contentment in what we receive—as long as our care plan is not compromised.

Discipline plays a key role in maintaining consistency within a holistic and structured care plan. This includes regular exercise, proper nutrition and medication, social interactions, adequate hydration, and other daily practices that we, as seniors, must stay mindful of.
It's also worth noting that these lifestyle habits are not optional; they become essential parts of our daily routine. So, who says we seniors have all the time in the world to simply relax? Yes, there is joy in leisure, but only when we effectively manage our time and stay committed to aging gracefully.

In my earlier book, *Let Your Organs Breathe*, I explored the deep interconnection between the body, mind, and soul, highlighting the role of diet and exercise in supporting holistic wellness, especially as we age. By embracing this integrated approach, we cultivate self-awareness, which in turn empowers us to make mindful choices that nurture our health, vitality, and sense of purpose.

While current technology cannot stop the ageing process, it *can* help us shape our ageing journey navigating it with dignity, purpose, peace, and happiness.

Ageing gracefully is not the closing of a chapter, but the opening of a new one—and our best is yet to come.

With my heartfelt gratitude, I invite you to pause and ask yourself: *What does ageing gracefully mean to me—and what small steps can I begin today to truly live it?*